Praise for *What To Do If...?*

'Anne-Maartje Oud is the world's leading expert on human behaviour and communication.' RADIM PAŘÍK, PRESIDENT OF ASSOCIATION OF NEGOTIATORS

'Practical, insightful and relevant to any workplace.' THIERRY TOMASIN MCA, RESTAURANT DIRECTOR

'A practical, inspiring book, full of useful advice for anyone building their career.' ANGELIQUE DERWORT, GLOBAL SENIOR HR VICE PRESIDENT

'This book gets straight to the real challenges professionals run into. If you want a resource that helps you navigate real workplace challenges without unnecessary theory or filler, this is a book worth having within reach. Pick it up, go to the chapter that matches the situation you're dealing with, and put the guidance into practice. It's that usable.' LIZ BADGLEY, SENIOR SECURITY PROGRAMME MANAGER

What To Do If...?

How to handle any situation at work and come out winning

Anne-Maartje Oud

Publisher's note

Every possible effort has been made to ensure that the information contained in this book is accurate at the time of going to press, and the publishers and author cannot accept responsibility for any errors or omissions, however caused. No responsibility for loss or damage occasioned to any person acting, or refraining from action, as a result of the material in this publication can be accepted by the editor, the publisher or the author.

First published in Great Britain and the United States in 2026 by Kogan Page Limited

All rights reserved. No part of this publication may be reproduced, stored or transmitted by any means without prior written permission from Kogan Page, except as permitted under applicable copyright laws.

Kogan Page
Kogan Page Ltd, 2nd Floor, 45 Gee Street, London EC1V 3RS, United Kingdom
Kogan Page Inc, 8 W 38th Street, Suite 902, New York, NY 10018, USA
www.koganpage.com

EU Representative (GPSR)
eucomply OÜ, Pärnu mnt 139b -14 11317, Tallinn, Estonia
www.eucompliancepartner.com

Kogan Page books are printed on paper from sustainable forests.

© Anne-Maartje Oud, 2026

The moral rights of the author have been asserted in accordance with the Copyright, Designs and Patents Act 1988.

ISBNs
Hardback   978 1 3986 2618 8
Paperback   978 1 3986 2616 4
Ebook   978 1 3986 2617 1

British Library Cataloguing-in-Publication Data
A CIP record for this book is available from the British Library.

Library of Congress Cataloging-in-Publication Data
A CIP record for this book is available from the Library of Congress.

Typeset by Integra Software Services, Pondicherry
Printed and bound by CPI Group (UK) Ltd, Croydon CR0 4YY

Contents

Preface viii
Acknowledgements xi

Introduction 1

PART ONE
Self-development 13

1 What to do if I want to change my behaviour? 15
2 What to do if I want to enhance my introspection? 20
3 What to do if I want to enhance my self-discipline? 27
4 What to do if I want to enhance my self-presentation? 33
5 What to do if I want to boost my confidence? 40
6 What to do if I want to practise new behaviour and stay true to myself? 46
7 What to do if I want to get out of my comfort zone? 53

PART TWO
Communication 61

8 What to do if I don't know where to put my hands in a presentation? 63
9 What to do if I have to prepare for a presentation? 70
10 What to do if I'm nervous about a presentation? 78
11 What to do if I need to attend a networking meeting? 85
12 What to do if I am looking for the most significant nonverbal cues? 91
13 What to do if I want to have effective conversations? 96
14 What to do if I want to become better at online meetings? 102

PART THREE
Working with others 109

15 What to do if I want to give feedback to my colleague? 111
16 What to do if I want to become better at observing others? 120
17 What to do if I want to connect with coworkers? 126
18 What to do if someone is belittling me? 132
19 What to do if your colleague or employee keeps making excuses? 139
20 What to do if someone doesn't respond? 146
21 What to do if I want to become a better listener? 153

PART FOUR
Leadership 159

22 What to do if you are starting a new job as a leader? 161
23 What to do if I need to conduct a meeting? 168
24 What to do if I want to be more approachable? 174
25 What to do if people don't want to participate in a meeting? 183
26 What to do if people don't do what they are supposed to do? 190
27 What to do if I want to become a more trustworthy leader? 199
28 What to do if you're leading a diverse team with different needs, preferences and cultural backgrounds? 207

PART FIVE
Difficult situations 215

29 What to do if someone is crying? 217
30 What to do if someone is angry and I need to de-escalate a situation? 223

31 What to do if I don't want to hire toxic people? 231
32 What to do if I work with someone who has narcissistic traits? 239
33 What to do if I work with a colleague with paranoid traits? 246
34 What to do if I work with a colleague who is emotionally unstable? 253
35 What to do if I want to communicate nonverbally in a difficult conversation? 260

Conclusion 266

Afterword 269
References 270
Further reading 273

Preface

Throughout my years of advising, teaching and training in the workplace, I've been asked many questions by a variety of people. Surprisingly, many of them boil down to the same thing: 'What would you advise me to do if...?' followed by their specific scenario. They ask for a practical and applicable advice regarding behaviour that they can use in that scenario.

Questions that focus on how to influence others, present yourself effectively, gain acceptance, be understood and lead. People ask about how they should interact with their friends as well as how they should interact with their colleagues; they confide in me the problems they run into at work and sometimes discover there is an overlap with situations they encounter at home. It all comes down to their need to show effective behaviour for the situation at hand. People want to know how to get things done and how to navigate unknown or difficult situations.

Although 'what to do if...' questions were asked to me in many forms and settings, in this book I'm focusing on questions asked within business situations. Over the course of my 20 years in this field, these 35 questions have been most frequently asked. For each question, I've provided seven strategies to tackle the problem at hand, providing you with a variety of solutions so you can choose and work with multiple options. You don't need to read this book from beginning to end. It's designed as a practical guide, so you can start with any question that matters to you and feel free to jump back and forth as needed. You might come across some repetition now and then, but that's intentional, as some strategies apply to more than one situation.

Furthermore, the strategies discussed have not only been conceptualized during coaching sessions but have also been put into practice in real-life scenarios, where they have proven to be effective. People have used them on the job and got great results.

Of course, there are many more strategies out there, but I've chosen this selection for their effectiveness and relevance in professional practice. Some may resonate more than others, but I encourage you to explore them all with curiosity. Reflect on your own situation and consider which strategies might resonate most with you. But do me a favour and don't ditch them all before you've tried them. Because what I see in my line of work is that the best results come from DOING. Don't over analyse, don't dismiss it immediately. Just go and try them out. Get out of your comfort zone and work with it.

There are five parts to the book, focusing on different questions with an underlying theme.

Part One is all about self-development, because that's where everything begins. It's about looking at yourself, knowing your qualities and pitfalls and figuring out how to get better. We'll explore questions and strategies to help you improve different parts of yourself.

Part Two zooms in on communication. It covers how to handle yourself in meetings, presentations and common office situations. You'll find tips on improving your communication skills to make a better impression at work.

Part Three focuses on working with others. This part will break down ways to better connect, communicate and collaborate with your colleagues. Whether it's overcoming common hurdles or just finding your way in a group, we'll explore some strategies on how to make teamwork a lot more effective.

Part Four delves deeper into leadership, exploring the traits and actions that can help you become a better leader, with tips and advice on how to step up your leadership game, whether you're leading a team for the first time or looking to improve your skills.

Part Five goes into the difficult situations you might encounter. A trigger warning is in order for this part, as it goes into the harsher and more uncomfortable conversations and situations that might happen at work.

I wish you a wonderful reading experience, but more importantly, I wish you the energy to put things into practice. As you read this book, don't just absorb the information. Try things out. Give yourself that little nudge in the right direction. You'll be amazed at what you can achieve!

Acknowledgements

A heartfelt thanks to my mentor Joe Navarro, who taught me numerous valuable things. His brilliant mind and unwavering support have been invaluable on this journey.

A big thank you to Rein, Erna, Karen, Walter, Lily, Rosie and Nicole for being there and opening up your homes and hearts. And to all my other friends who, without knowing I was writing this book, supported me with their spirit, conversations, nights out and joy – your contributions were invaluable. Hanneke and Victor, Danny, Irene, Ilse, Annemijn, Pia, Catelijne, Mirjam and Frank, Mi, Marloes, a big warm thank you. Thank you, Willeke, Diana, Poppy, Sander and Sander, Malou, Joost, Ryan, Olivier and Martijn, for your support throughout the process. Much appreciated!

Antonio de Luca, connecting others is your most extraordinary quality and, one day, you'll connect the whole world.

And most importantly, I want to thank all the clients who have put their trust in me, particularly those with whom I've worked since 2006 under the banner of The Behaviour Company. Your commitment, determination, drive and eagerness to enhance your behaviour have been the inspiration for this book. I hope it inspires others to follow in your footsteps.

Introduction

My passion for enhancing others' behaviour skills began in 1998 when I graduated from the Academy of Arts in the Netherlands with a degree in dramatic expression through word and gesture. Initially, I saw myself as a director, actor and teacher. However, it took me a few years to fully grasp what I had truly learned. In the end I realized that I am, above all, a trained observer. I have been trained to closely observe and listen to people and then to assist them in improving.

When I started to find out this other world of business instead of art, I was hooked. Doesn't everybody know about how to be on a stage? Don't they know what a pause can do? What the effect of eye contact can be? What a smile can do, or a frown?

I decided to fully leave the world of art behind and focus on business. And I loved it. With every assignment I took I learned more. Of course I studied extra after my graduation. Many things. I learned about group dynamics, communication, how humans adapt, grow and learn, the development of the human brain and many more things. One of my best teachers was and still is Joe Navarro. I had the honour to work on a five-year mentorship and graduated with honours when I completed the instructor programme, both in Behavioural and Dangerous Personality Assessment as well as Nonverbal Communication. Joe is a living encyclopaedia with almost all the knowledge in the world. Or at least, it came across that way. A lot of people know him as a nonverbal communication specialist, but he also taught me about toxic personalities, history, politics, nature and all his experiences within the FBI (if he was allowed to talk about it, of course). All these topics are important for understanding humans and knowing more about our species.

His mission for me: 'Now go and apply this knowledge to your clients, because that's what you do best. Working with people and making it practical.'

That's been my goal throughout my entire career, even before meeting Joe. I've always strived to help people discover new workplace behaviours that they hadn't considered before and help them reach their professional (and sometimes personal) objectives. My approach focuses on finding actions that match people's goals and tackling behaviours that get in the way. I also train these people in new behaviours. I help them reach their objectives more easily with specified targeted behaviour.

It can be a very small idea or a very small change in your behaviour that can help you to reach your goals. Other times it's much harder for people to become effective and the trajectories to enhance their behaviour take longer. But in the end, it's about the will to become more effective.

If you are that person who wants to become more effective... this book will help you with that.

People often don't realize just how much they're capable of; you have a whole range of behaviours you can tap into. Think of your behaviour like a painter's palette. You might prefer certain colours, but sometimes it's helpful and exciting to try something new. It might feel a bit strange or awkward at first, but once you see what you can create, you might end up loving that new 'colour'; a behaviour you didn't even know you had in you. As a behavioural advisor, I get to help people discover and enhance those new sides of themselves.

People crave practical advice, something they can immediately apply to their situations. I've found that people are truly grateful when provided with actionable steps tailored to their needs. This book aims to do just that.

All I ask is that you don't keep this information to yourself. Share it with others and help them realize the power of adopting new behaviours and strategies for increased effectiveness.

Some ground principles

To master behaviour at work, I want to share four essential principles with you. These principles are incredibly important to me and are the foundation of The Behaviour Company. They are central to everything we do and teach and are crucial for enhancing workplace interactions and fostering a positive, productive environment. I believe you can't do anything effectively without considering these foundational principles. By keeping these principles in mind, you'll find it easier to apply all the strategies you encounter in this book.

These principles come from years of experience and countless interactions. When you use them, you transform how you tackle challenges and you will seize opportunities at work. You will learn more about them as you progress through the book, but, for now, here's a brief overview in this chapter.

Principle 1: 'The best conversations take place with comfort for both parties'

In any situation involving interaction, it's essential to remember that there are multiple parties involved. I often see people forgetting this crucial aspect. It's a common mistake to overlook the fact that communication involves more than just one person. When someone has something they want to share, they can become so focused on their own perspective that they neglect the other party's feelings. They are so driven by the need to get their message across that they are expecting the other person to listen with full attention, while bringing their own emotions into the conversation, without considering how it might affect the other person. This often results in statements like, 'You should listen to me', 'You need to fix this' or 'You need to focus on me', or it manifests in their behaviour – such as speaking in long monologues without taking the other person into account.

The reverse can happen too. Sometimes, a conversation is entirely focused on the other person, prioritizing their happiness and being fully attentive to their needs, while forgetting that you yourself have feelings, needs and goals in the conversation as well. For example, in a meeting with a dissatisfied client, you see people focusing entirely on addressing the concerns, agreeing to all the clients' requests to keep them happy. They might say things like, 'We'll take care of everything', or nod along without expressing any reservations, all to avoid conflict. In doing so, you might neglect your own company's needs, such as budget constraints or resource limitations, setting unrealistic expectations that could strain your team's capacity and jeopardize the project.

If one of the above happens, the balance is off and if we want to have effective conversations, we need comfort for both parties.

Comfort allows each person to express their thoughts and feelings without fear of judgment. If we can create comfort for both parties, all will feel free to ask questions, clarify uncertainties and engage fully in the conversation. That will lead to better understanding and clearer communication.

When both parties feel heard and respected, you will see that it enhances mutual trust and cooperation, making it easier to find common ground and resolve issues. This means that you have to take care of yourself as well as the needs of that other person. It means reflecting on your own comfort as well as theirs, asking yourself: What do I need and what does the other person need?

Principle 2: 'Know your role, know your goal'

Both your role and goal are important to define how you will position yourself in the conversation. If we first focus on 'know your role', it means you must understand that it's crucial in defining your position in the conversation. Understanding your role means recognizing the identity you bring to the discussion. For example, giving feedback to your child is completely different from being a manager giving feedback to a colleague. Defining your role is essential, as it might even mean you shouldn't have that difficult conversation at all. For instance, you might decide it's not appropriate in your role to give feedback to a client.

Also, consider your goal. You should be aware why are you having that specific conversation in the first place. Are you speaking impulsively, driven by heightened emotions and the need to vent, or would it be better to pause, take a deep breath and consider the long-term implications of your words? Your goals could be to express your emotions, negotiate with a client or motivate your team. All different goals that call for a different approach. Once you've defined your goal, make sure you stick to it during the conversation and avoid deviating from it if possible.

Principle 3: 'The key to effective communication is observation'

Observation is crucial in effective conversations. Through observation, you can get so much information. You really need to look at the other person and observe the signals they are giving you. If you don't, you are missing essential nonverbal cues. I see this often in my line of work where people prepare, write things down and then just stare at the paper in front of them, failing to make eye contact. Or they stare at a computer screen instead of connecting with the person in front of them.

It's important to observe the other person, but also to be aware of yourself. Self-observation can give you cues as well. Ask yourself questions like, 'Am I comfortable enough? Is my voice too loud? What is my behaviour? What am I doing? What am I portraying?' Because only with this self-observation are you able to adjust the things that are needed to make the conversation more effective.

Principle 4: 'Apply the Helicopter Metaphor Technique'

The fourth principle would be applying the Helicopter Metaphor Technique to your conversations. This technique helps you take a step back, gain perspective and approach any conversation, whether difficult or routine, with clarity and awareness.

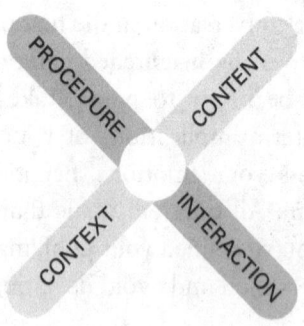

INTRODUCTION

I've been working with the Helicopter Metaphor Technique for many years and it serves as a central concept I use to explain how to navigate and be conscious in difficult conversations. In 2020, I shared the concept with Joe Navarro and we wrote about it together in *Psychology Today*. That article introduced the metaphor to a broader audience. What I want to do here is give it a bit more space to explain what it means, how it works in practice and why it's such a helpful tool in moments that ask a lot of us.

It works with the basis of four components within conversations: **Context, Procedure, Content** and **Interaction**. All these four need to be observed, understood and navigated during a conversation.

Context matters because without understanding what's really happening, in the company, in politics, in the economy, you risk having a conversation that sounds right but misses the point completely. Imagine that, for instance, budgets have just been cut, people have lost their jobs and you're asking for a raise without acknowledging any of that. It's not just tone deaf; it shows you're not tuned in to the environment around you. And that affects how your message lands. You need to be aware of the wider circumstances in which the conversation is happening.

The **Procedure** covers the more practical things. It's all those things like where the conversation takes place, how long it lasts, how much time you have and when it happens. A Monday morning is different from a Friday afternoon. A five-minute chat is not the same as a three-hour meeting. These may seem like simple details, but they really shape a conversation. The timing, duration and setting influences the way people behave in conversation and the outcome it has.

Content is everything that is said during a conversation. It is almost like minutes in a meeting, essentially – the transcript of the verbal words. It doesn't include how something is said or what is left unsaid, just the literal words.

And last, but not least, **Interaction**. This is often revealed more in posture and presence and it's all about the behaviour: what is the tone, what do we see happening with body language and what nonverbal cues are being exchanged between the people involved? You can look at how people behave towards one another or within a group. You look at what nonverbal signals are being given and picked up and you pay attention to power dynamics, unspoken hierarchies and the way influence moves through the group.

You need these four elements as a reference when you are in the middle of a conversation to identify if you are having an effective conversation. When we use the Helicopter Metaphor Technique, we can see these four themes as the blades keeping the helicopter in motion: they are what propel the conversation forward. And just like the blades, they need to be noticed and balanced at all times (see Figure 2).

The Helicopter Metaphor Technique is a helpful image in those moments when you feel like you are not making progress, when feelings are overwhelming or emotions start to dominate. In those moments when you feel something different is needed, let that image of the helicopter act as a nudge to get you back on track.

Using the Helicopter Metaphor Technique is like being a pilot in conversation. You should be able to navigate, observe and adjust when something feels off. When you sense the conversation needs a shift, the metaphor reminds you that in challenging moments, agility and perspective are key to changing the course of a conversation and to helping yourself to get out of that difficult moment when you might seem to be stuck. You don't need to stay fixed on one path; you can use the skills below. The way a pilot can navigate a helicopter is the way you can navigate a conversation:

1 **Flight agility:** One of the most powerful things about a helicopter is its agility. It can move in any direction: up, down, sideways, even hover in place, and it doesn't need a

runway. It's built for adaptability. And that's exactly the mindset we need in difficult conversations. Agility means you're not stuck; you can move, shift perspective and change direction. Flight agility is the ability to shift, adapt and change when the conversation calls for it.

2 **Precise yet delicate steering:** All the controls work together in a helicopter and they're very sensitive. Flying one takes full focus and coordination. You need both hands and both feet and a calm, steady presence to make even the smallest adjustments. It requires a high level of coordination, focus and constant adjustment. The same goes for navigating a difficult conversation. It asks for attention, precision and presence. Your mind should be clear and focused, your phone off, your desk free of distractions. Your body language matters and should be engaged as well. It's the subtle moves that make the difference in the conversation.

3 **Flying high:** If you feel stuck, remind yourself: I can lift up and get a broader view to see what is happening. Flying high gives you a broader perspective. Like a helicopter surveying the landscape, you take in the full picture. You observe what is happening. You notice body language, tone, energy, words, emotions, the setting. All the four elements need focus. What happens with context, procedure, content and interaction. This wide-angle view helps you identify patterns and connections. Just like a pilot you need a sense of the bigger picture before you decide where to go next.

4 **Flying low:** This one comes in when a word, a reaction or a shift in tone catches your attention, which could be a cue for you to slow down and explore. Flying low is about zooming in and taking a closer look at something that stands out in the conversation. What feels important here? What might be underneath? For example, someone might casually say, 'Well, I just have to survive this quarter', and then move on. That word 'survive' might signal something deeper. Ask questions like, 'What do you mean by that? or 'Can you tell me more?'

or 'I noticed your tone changed, do you recognize that?' Just like when a helicopter flying low reveals details, this part of the conversation is where you look and listen with scrutiny.

5. **Hovering:** A helicopter can hover in place, remaining almost completely still in the air. In a conversation, you can hover for a moment to think. Hovering gives you that extra time to observe and analyse more deeply. When you use this technique, you pause and don't say anything. You listen, watch and observe, but you do not act. You build situational awareness, taking in what's happening around you, assessing calmly, choosing your next move with care. Even if the conversation isn't moving forward just yet, your presence, your clarity and your ability to stay steady is progress. You stay engaged, but you don't lose yourself in turbulence.

6. **Flying backwards:** Sometimes during a conversation you realize it's worth taking a step back to return to something that was said earlier. For example, someone might have said early on, 'This whole project has felt off from the beginning'. The conversation moves on, but that sentence stays with you. Later, you can pause and say, 'You mentioned earlier that the project felt off from the beginning; can you tell me more about that?' By circling back, you invite them to go deeper into something they may have brushed past. Just like flying a helicopter, sometimes you need to turn around and revisit the spot that needs a closer look.

7. **Getting out of the helicopter:** Just because you can push through a hard conversation doesn't always mean it's wise to do so. Sometimes, you wait for better conditions. Just like flying a helicopter, a meaningful conversation shouldn't take place in a stormy environment. A noisy office, constant interruptions or a lack of privacy can make it hard to concentrate or connect. When that happens, you don't have to force it to go on. You land. You pause and choose a better setting. Maybe that means going for a walk, stepping into a quieter room or finding a space where both people feel more

at ease. You're still having the conversation but you're doing it in a place that supports more presence and focus. Because just like flying, the conditions around you matter. The right conversation needs the right space.

8 **Flying away:** As the pilot in the conversation, you also have the choice not to take passengers on board. Some conversations need a pause altogether. Maybe emotions are running high, maybe you're not feeling clear-headed or maybe the timing is simply off. You can suggest taking a break, grabbing a coffee or rescheduling the conversation entirely. You don't have to push through just because it started. Flying away doesn't mean avoiding; it means choosing the right moment to re-engage with more clarity, calm and intention.

9 **Limiting baggage:** Sometimes, you notice that emotional baggage is weighing heavily on the conversation. There's too much focus on the past, on what's been said, done or left unresolved. Just like a helicopter can't lift off when it's carrying too much weight, a conversation can't move forward when it's overloaded with unresolved emotion. That includes your own. Be aware of the weight you're bringing into the conversation and be mindful about what the other person might be carrying too. Has the tension been building for hours, days or even months? Before real progress can happen, it often helps to acknowledge what's there and, when possible, begin to lighten the load by addressing it.

10 **Chart the course:** Charting the course means planning a direction for where you want to go and how you'll get there. It starts before the conversation when you are thinking ahead about your intention, your timing and the outcome you hope to reach. But it doesn't stop there. After the conversation, you still have to navigate. Perhaps that means following up, gathering more information or doing what you said you would do. Charting the course, before and after, keeps you clear, steady and focused.

Conclusion

All these principles will help you build stronger relationships, communicate better and reach your goals. Remember, mastering behaviour is a journey and these principles are your guide along the way.

PART ONE

Self-development

Everything begins with self-development. When we are able to reflect on ourselves and recognize the impact we have on others, we can start to grow. It is only when you understand the impact you have on others and why you have that impact on others that you can identify areas where you might need to change, adapt or improve. It takes courage to engage in self-reflection, as it is not always easy to look at yourself with honesty.

Many books emphasize the idea that you are good enough as you are and while I fully agree that self-love is important, there's something truly powerful about striving to grow and develop. Along the way, you'll come across aspects of yourself that may be uncomfortable to confront and it takes effort to educate yourself and it requires stamina to change your behaviour.

By continuously analysing and practising new behaviours you begin to generate change. If you're willing to commit to this process and align it with your inner self and goals, you'll go far.

This part focuses on the importance of self-reflection, building confidence and practising new behaviours to drive personal growth. It explores practical strategies to enhance your self-development, helping you become more adaptable and confident. By consistently analysing your actions and pushing yourself to try new approaches, you can grow. Step outside of your comfort zone and nudge yourself to embrace unfamiliar challenges. Because bravery is crucial for development.

CHAPTER ONE

What to do if I want to change my behaviour?

It's not always easy to change your behaviour, but a lot of benefit can come from it. If you recognize the need to change your behaviour, congratulations. It means that either you've done some self-reflection, or you have taken feedback from others seriously.

I personally don't use the word 'change' very often. I see it as tweaking and fine-tuning existing behaviours. You are a grown-up and you've survived so far. Your current behaviour must be effective, but with some adjustments, it can be optimized for even better interactions and outcomes.

It might be that you want to enhance your time management, your presentation skills, your leadership style; in essence, it doesn't matter. The principles behind making a change are all pretty much the same, no matter what area you're focusing on. The most important thing is to stay committed to the process, be kind and patient with yourself along the way and just keep practising consistently. Every little bit of improvement, even the smallest progress, adds up and contributes to your overall growth and success in the long run. Plus, the positive changes you make can have a ripple effect, inspiring the people around you and encouraging them to make improvements in their own lives as well.

When you're able to change your behaviour successfully, it can really give your confidence and self-esteem a huge boost. I've seen so many people beaming with pride after reaching their goals, whether it's giving a presentation, saying no to the boss or becoming more punctual. The effect it has on them is really powerful, giving them this amazing sense of strength and accomplishment they didn't even know they had in them.

Learning to adapt and being able to change your behaviour makes you stronger and more capable of the situations that you will encounter in the workplace. So, what are some strategies that you can use in that process?

Strategy 1: Identify the reason you want to change

Really knowing why you want to change and focusing on the positive outcome once you have changed will help you in the process. Knowing your reasons makes it easier than just doing something for the sake of it. Imagine how the change will improve your life and the benefits it will bring. Visualization can help you stay focused and motivated. Some people write down their goals with a clear reason behind them, while others create mood boards or visualize a specific image. Focusing on the rewards, like securing a new position, getting a raise or landing a new job, can also be a powerful motivator.

Strategy 2: Set clear goals

Define clear, achievable goals for the behaviour change you want to make. What is it that you want to change? Writing down your goals clearly can be very helpful. For example, 'I want to give a presentation with a clear voice and a compelling story', or 'I want to say no to my manager in a way that they accept it and I feel strong and confident'.

Sometimes you can break these goals into smaller, manageable steps to make the process. A presentation for your team might be less overwhelming than an immediate presentation for a client. Your goal could be:

> I want to improve my public speaking skills so I can present to the client in three months. I will watch at least three TED Talks and YouTube videos in the next three weeks. I will practise every other day and schedule a presentation with my colleague, asking her for feedback this month. I will write scripts and create slides within one month with help from my boss. I will present weekly, review the recordings and implement specific improvements based on feedback for the next three months.

Strategy 3: Find support from others

Share your goals with someone you trust, who can hold you accountable. Regular check-ins with this person can provide support and encouragement. That way you can build a support network around you that is important for your journey. In the Netherlands, there is a beautiful ad aimed at people who want to quit smoking (Blom, 2023). It's presented from the perspective of the smokers, who ask for understanding and support from their family and loved ones. 'I need you to believe in me and trust that I am doing my best.' Once we have support from others, we can accomplish things we'd never imagined.

Surround yourself with supportive people who encourage your growth and hold you accountable. When you are sharing your journey with others it can provide the motivation and assistance you need.

Strategy 4: Stay committed

Changing behaviour takes time and effort. It's not easy; it's about falling and getting back up. Changing your behaviour can profoundly impact both your personal and professional life.

When I work with people on changing their behaviour, some become very frustrated if they can't succeed within the first three attempts. However, the best part is that if they persevere and keep trying, it eventually works. A manager whom I coached a few years ago recently told me he is very happy that the results have lasted. Even though he didn't believe it would work at first, patience and perseverance proved to be a virtue.

Stay committed to your goals and be patient with yourself. Remember that setbacks are normal, but persistence is key.

Strategy 5: Track progress

Sometimes it's helpful not to focus solely on the end goal but to monitor your progress regularly. Rewarding yourself for making progress can boost your motivation and reinforce positive behaviour changes. I've kept a to-do book for a while, tracking all the tasks I completed toward a bigger goal. Whenever I felt frustrated about not reaching the goal yet, I found joy in seeing how much I had already accomplished. Step by step. You can keep a journal or use a tracking app to record your efforts and achievements. This will help you stay motivated and identify areas where you may need to adjust your approach.

Strategy 6: Be kind

You have to be kind to yourself throughout the process. Practise self-compassion, because the critical voices in your head are usually not effective. While they can sometimes nudge you into action, they are often harsh and negative. Many people I guide remain inactive because they tell themselves, 'I can't do it', 'It's been done before' or 'I'm not good enough'. That's not helpful at all. Understand that change is challenging and it's okay to make mistakes. Learn from the mistakes and move forward without self-judgment. It's much more helpful to think, 'I'm doing the best I can. I'm making progress. Look at me being a badass for trying!'

Strategy 7: Educate and train yourself

Read books, attend workshops or seek professional advice to gain a deeper understanding of the behaviour you want to change. Knowledge can empower you to make more informed decisions. Practising helps you build muscle memory in new behaviours. I often work with actors to help people practise new behaviours, such as handling difficult conversations. Once you've practised skills in a safe setting, it's less intimidating to apply them in real life. You can ask the actor to display a certain behaviour you find challenging and work with both the actor and trainer to refine your response. Although the practice situation may not be exactly the same as real life, your body and brain will have already experienced something similar. This helps build confidence and familiarity, making it easier to handle the conversation when it happens for real.

Conclusion

While changing behaviour is not easy and often challenging, it is certainly doable with commitment and perseverance. Remember that each small step forward is progress. Celebrate your successes, no matter how small. With dedication, you can achieve your goals and see significant improvements over time.

CHAPTER TWO

What to do if I want to enhance my introspection?

Self-development and enhancing yourself begins with introspection. It's not always easy to look in the mirror and honestly assess our own qualities and shortcomings. It's important to recognize that we all have flaws and others may find it challenging to work with us just as we find it challenging to work with them. When people seek advice from me on how to deal with difficult individuals, I often pose a question: 'What makes you difficult yourself?' Understanding our strengths and weaknesses not only provides insight during interactions with others but also highlights what makes us unique. What sets you apart? What makes you a collaborative team member, or how do you contribute to a project or work setting? It's essential to recognize our own identity and the impact we have on those around us. You can do that through self-reflection.

It's about paying attention to your thoughts, emotions and actions. By reflecting on them, you get a better sense of who you are. Sometimes you can even reflect on the reasons behind your way of interacting with others. For example, was it something you learned from your former teachers, shaped by the expectations of your previous company, or influenced by the values of your family?

It can help you understand why you feel a certain way or why you react to situations in specific manners. This introspection allows us to understand ourselves better and it can help us to identify both strengths and areas for improvement. We can uncover patterns and motivations that may not be immediately obvious and offer us the chance to adjust our behaviours for more positive outcomes.

Strategy 1: Take your time

Reflection requires time and a personalized approach. Personally, I've found that it naturally occurs during moments like driving home after a workday or when I am enjoying a lazy Sunday on the couch. However, it's also possible to structure reflection into your schedule. You could set aside dedicated time each day or week to reflect on your thoughts, feelings and experiences. You can integrate it into your morning or evening routine, or reserve moments of downtime at the end of the week.

For example, I once worked with a manager who I advised to make it a habit to reflect every Friday. He would review his agenda, assess how the week went, tasks to focus on in the coming week, acknowledge his accomplishments and interactions with others and identify areas for improvement. Additionally, he paid attention to his energy levels and made sure he felt good about wrapping up the week.

Similarly, another manager I know opted to take a long walk with her dog every Sunday as a dedicated time for reflection. During these walks, she would assess how she felt about the week and herself, essentially taking her emotional and mental 'temperature'.

Taking time off for a holiday can also give you the space to reflect on what's happening in your life. We've all had those 'aha' moments after stepping away from work for a bit.

Strategy 2: Write things down

It's easy to get caught up in your thoughts, so writing down your thoughts, emotions and observations in a journal can be incredibly helpful. Some find it beneficial to write things down just before bed as they reflect on their day. Personally, I prefer to write when I've had an especially good day, when I'm feeling proud of myself, or when I've had a great time and want to remember specific details. You can write about your day, your interactions with others, questions you may have or any insights you've gained about yourself. You can reflect on your progress towards specific goals, writing down both your achievements and the obstacles you've faced. Maybe you notice a pattern in how you react to certain situations or discover a hidden strength you hadn't fully recognized.

Strategy 3: Ask questions

Challenge yourself with questions that encourage deeper self-reflection and insight. There are fantastic books available to assist you with reflection and journaling. One example is *999 Questions to Ask Yourself* (BBNC Uitgevers, 2019), which offers a fun and insightful way to delve into self-discovery and introspection. In the Netherlands, we even have a tea brand that adds questions to each teabag label, offering little moments of reflection. You'll come across questions like, 'What does your perfect day look like?' or 'What's your dream job?' – a gentle way to pause and think. However, a more formal approach involves asking yourself meaningful questions that resonate with you.

Questions like, 'What kind of impact do I want to have on the people around me?' or 'What skills do I want to develop or improve?' can prompt deep self-reflection and help clarify your values. In coaching sessions, I often guide individuals to explore such questions to uncover underlying reasons behind ineffective behaviours or negative interactions with others. 'Why do I do what I do? What might be the reason? What are the benefits and what are the pitfalls?' In essence, this practice is about having a conversation with yourself – where you're both the speaker and the listener. It's a chance to get to know yourself better and consciously guide your path of growth.

Strategy 4: Reflect after meetings or presentations

When you have back-to-back meetings, a lot of people forget that taking time out for reflection is key for learning and self-development. It's very beneficial to assess your performance after a meeting by asking yourself what went smoothly, what could have been better and how you can enhance your approach next time. You can mentally replay the meeting, or you can focus on specific interactions to gain insights for improvement. I like to rate my performance on a scale from 1 to 10, with 10 being the highest (which I never score because according to me there's always room to improve). When I score lower than an 8, I know something's up. I don't just think about how I performed; I dig deeper into what's going on in my life. Could it have been my preparation or perhaps factors like my energy level or mood that day? As a bit of a perfectionist, I've learned through reflection and introspection that, as much as I'd love to hit a perfect 10 every time, perfection is impossible. Looking back and reflecting is a great way to grow, both personally and professionally, helping you keep evolving and adapting.

Strategy 5: Ask others for feedback

Asking for feedback provides valuable insights. Discussing the meeting or your performance with others can be helpful. 'What were their observations? How do others perceive you? What would they advise you to improve? What is the effect of your behaviour on them and does that align with your own beliefs about yourself?' Their comments or assessments allow you to gain different perspectives on your actions and interactions. Once you receive the feedback, take the time to sit with that information and reflect on it. Consider whether you recognize the aspects of yourself that others have highlighted. Ask yourself if you would describe yourself in the same way they do. If there is a difference this process of self-reflection can lead to a deeper understanding of how you are perceived by others and help you identify areas for personal growth and improvement.

Strategy 6: Read, watch and learn

Engaging with books, articles, podcasts, videos and conversations with others who have valuable insights can provide fresh perspectives and new ideas for self-reflection and development. One particular book I recommend is *Be Exceptional* by Joe Navarro, as it offers valuable insights into improving oneself as a person. In his book, Joe presents five fundamental traits that can assist anyone in reaching their full potential and achieving excellence in different areas of life: Self-Mastery, Observation, Communication, Action and Psychological Comfort.

The book serves as a practical guide, inspiring and motivating individuals to pursue personal growth and self-improvement.

Movies can also be powerful tools for self-reflection. Take, for example, two of my favourite films: *The Truman Show* and *American Beauty*. In *The Truman Show*, we see the main character as he discovers his world is not real and that he's part of a TV show. It makes you wonder: do we possess Truman's level of awareness about our own lives? Are we sharp observers who truly see what is around us?

On the other hand, *American Beauty* challenges you to examine your life choices and goals. It's set against a suburban setting and could inspire you to think about your choices of what truly makes you happy. *Revolutionary Road*, another great movie, with Kate Winslet and Leonardo di Caprio, also focuses on that theme. It explores themes of struggle between personal aspirations and societal expectations.

More than just sources of entertainment, films like these can help us to explore our inner selves. They encourage us to reflect on our life's choices and might prompt us to initiate change. They remind us that we have the possibility to reflect on our lives and make changes if needed, just like the main characters in these movies.

Strategy 7: Make decisions

Reflection for the sake of reflection is a waste of time. It's what you do with those reflections that truly matters. Think about what insights you've gained: what's in your power to change and what aspects of your life do you want to keep the same? It's turning those thoughts and insights into actions and decisions that makes you grow.

Through introspection, I realized that the challenge of maintaining social media presence demanded a lot of time and effort, which ultimately felt misaligned with my true self. Self-reflection helped me understand that constant visibility isn't something I want to put so much time and energy into. I chose to diligently do my work and let my actions speak for themselves and post what I like to post.

A client decided to start working fewer hours after reflecting that her work-life balance wasn't the way she wanted it to be. By reducing her hours by one day per month, it didn't affect her income too much, but it was really helpful for her to have an extra day off.

Conclusion

Self-reflection is about taking the time and effort to observe yourself and ask yourself questions, figuring out what really matters to you, and then using those insights to make choices that align with your goals. It's about understanding what drives you and matters in your life and then using that understanding to shape your behaviour accordingly. Instead of simply reacting to external circumstances, self-reflection empowers you to consciously choose actions and behaviours that are in line with your goals and purpose in life. So, instead of just going with the flow, you end up making decisions that genuinely reflect who you are and what you want out of life. It's a way to ensure you're not just reacting to what life throws at you but actively choosing behaviours that align with you.

CHAPTER THREE

What to do if I want to enhance my self-discipline?

It's not for everyone to work towards a particular goal. The positive side of a lack of discipline is flexibility. Going with the flow, so to say. But as a professional it's important that you are able to develop a skill of being focused and being able to deliver a text, a product or a presentation at a certain time.

If you're part of a company, you are not working alone. You have other people that are depending on you so you need to be that professional that can deliver. Maybe only certain artists don't have deadlines while they are creating masterpieces. It took Leonardo da Vinci an estimated 16 years to finish the *Mona Lisa*. He never completed several artworks and left many ideas unfinished on the drawing board. Unlike Leonardo, most of us need to follow deadlines to ensure productivity and progress.

Although creativity and flexibility are highly valued qualities, in a business setting, one of the most common complaints in teamwork is that others do not deliver what was promised, or they fail to deliver on time.

It might be hard to motivate yourself. It can be challenging on its own, but it gets even harder when you're tired, distracted or feeling nervous. So, what can you do to get things going?

Strategy 1: Set the stage

Some people work better with music in the background, some like it quieter. Some people can work for hours on end while others need a more pomodoro-style technique, where you work in focused blocks of 25 minutes followed by a five-minute break.

But whatever you do make sure that when you are focused you are not distracted by the little things in life. Turn your phone off and make sure it doesn't interrupt you. Even just seeing your phone might make you think of possible messages or other things you must do.

Make sure you have your drinks, snacks or all you need. It sounds trivial but when you prepare for your activity you will be focused more. This means mentally preparing: 'Yes I'm going to do this now.' But also, physical preparation is important: not being hungry, not being thirsty and not needing to go to the toilet while you are focusing on your task.

The room should help you as well. The lighting should be good, the temperature should be pleasant and the chair you sit in or desk you are working from should be comfortable. If you prefer some background noise, choose something you enjoy, like music from your Spotify list. There are even playlists specifically for concentration and studying. Some people might find it nice to hear chatter in the background, perhaps at their favourite coffee shop.

If there's distracting noise, use noise-cancelling headphones. They are much more pleasant than dealing with construction work outside, a crying baby or loud traffic.

Strategy 2: Make a plan that works for you

Are you a go-getter, do you start with a goal in mind and are you the person who makes sure everything else must give way for that goal? Or are you that person who needs free time as well? Time to unwind. To think. To do things step by step.

It's important to realize what your goal-orientated style is. First, I tried to write every day or every other day, but in the end, with my busy work I couldn't do that. Too little time, too much distraction. I found it much more effective to plan dedicated writing weeks. Sometimes, I would retreat with friends or family for a full week of writing. Other times, I took solo trips, staying in a hotel in London where I would write all day and then reward myself with dinner in that amazing city.

If you find yourself not working on your goal or not effectively working on your goal you are getting signals that you should change your approach.

Strategy 3: Create little goals

Some goals are huge. You might want to start your own company, or to clean out your office. It can overwhelm you. People can become almost paralysed by the amount of work they see ahead of them. The advice is to start with small steps that lead to bigger things. Everybody knows this, but they don't always apply it to their actual behaviour.

Break down larger tasks into smaller, manageable steps and set daily or weekly milestones. For example, you can divide writing a big report into sections to complete each day, such as the introduction on day one and chapter one on day two. Similarly, you can aim to finish specific tasks from your to-do list daily. I once advised a manager who was overwhelmed by his enormous to-do list to choose just three tasks to focus on each day. By focusing only on those three tasks first, he was more relaxed and with that less stressed approach he often finished quicker than expected. Any additional work done that day felt like a bonus.

Strategy 4: Reward yourself during the path

I once saw a great picture of a big folder filled with 850 pages of content that needed to be studied. The student who needed to learn the material had hidden a piece of chocolate every 75th page or so. And although I wouldn't recommend eating so much sugar, it's a nice way of nudging yourself through those hurdles of the pages. I once coached a lady who needed to rewrite a full business approach with rules and regulations. It would take her three months to get it done. Every Monday she would reflect on what she had already done and would treat herself with a walk in her favourite park. It became a ritual that helped her to clear her mind before starting the week.

Strategy 5: Reward yourself afterwards

If you achieve what you set out to do, make sure to celebrate. This doesn't mean you have to throw a big party; sometimes small celebrations can be meaningful as well. These marker moments help you acknowledge the goals you've set and accomplished. It could be as simple as enjoying a cup of coffee with a piece of cake or treating yourself to that nice shirt you've been eyeing.

In business cultures, where everyone is highly goal-oriented, taking time to celebrate wins is often overlooked. However, pausing to recognize your achievements has a significant positive effect. It helps you reflect on the steps you've taken to get where you are, whether it's a personal milestone or a team effort.

I once coached a woman who rewarded herself with a convertible after landing her long-desired managerial role. Although it was a bit above her budget, she made a conscious decision to go for it. She said, 'Every time I drive this car to work now, it reminds me of how well I did.'

Strategy 6: Talk about it with others

Trying to tackle everything on your own can be ineffective. You might be afraid of failing, which prevents you from doing what you need to do, or you may view the task as an overwhelming Mount Everest to climb. Sharing your goals and feelings with others can make a big difference. You can get advice, unload negative emotions and gain a new perspective. In coaching sessions, I've found that some people need to express their fear of failure and even cry about it. Afterwards, they often feel relieved and more relaxed, making it easier for them to start the task.

During these talks with others, you might also learn how they approach similar challenges. They can offer helpful tips on handling deadlines and large tasks. Working together not only makes tasks more manageable but also provides emotional support and practical solutions. Engaging with others can change your approach and make the journey less intimidating and more rewarding.

Strategy 7: Stop the excuses

All of the above might be excuses to avoid starting your task and doing what needs to be done. You might think, 'My office is too cold, so I can't do this now', or 'I don't have anything to eat, so I need to buy groceries first.' If you know you are prone to procrastination, make sure to nudge yourself and reflect on your own excuses. In the end, it all comes down to taking action.

One manager decided to lock himself in his office without a phone and asked his colleagues not to let him out for three hours so he could complete a task. This led to a hilarious situation when he needed to use the restroom, but they wouldn't let him out.

Conclusion

Staying focused and getting things done isn't always easy, especially with so many distractions around. But when you break it down, it's simpler than you might think. It's about figuring out what needs to get done and doing it. That part might sound easy, but the challenge is staying on track and not letting yourself get sidetracked.

Once you know what you need to do, take action. Don't overthink it or wait for the 'perfect time'. It's about pushing past any doubts or excuses and getting started. And sometimes, that's all it takes.

While it may sound straightforward, the key is to maintain that focus and discipline in the face of obstacles or temptations to procrastinate. It's about silencing the inner doubts and simply following through. As the iconic Nike slogan encourages us: 'Just Do It'.

CHAPTER FOUR

What to do if I want to enhance my self-presentation?

In this day and age, being socially active, presenting yourself and sharing personal experiences online are more important than ever. But also, in a work environment, letting others know who you are and what you've been up to is necessary and helpful to make yourself stand out and known to others.

While some may associate showing yourself with fashion choices and style considerations – like clothing, makeup and accessories – there's a broader perspective from a behavioural standpoint. From my behavioural perspective, there are many options beyond the superficial aspects. Those superficial aspects will help you, of course, but they are not all there is to go to.

A stylish new suit can certainly elevate your overall appearance, but the impact can be undone if you have a slouchy posture. Your nails might be perfect, but if you point your fingers at others like an angry schoolteacher you will be perceived negatively. The way you carry yourself plays a crucial role in showing confidence. It's not just about the attire; it's equally about how you wear it with confidence and poise.

When you understand how certain behaviours align with presenting yourself in a more confident way, it helps you to expand your choice in behaviour because your personal behaviour style can enhance your active self-presentation. During a podcast I once said: 'We are the sum total of our behaviours and communication and the effect it has on others'. This was inspired by Carl Sagan's quote: 'We are the sum of influence and impact that we have, in our lives, on others.'

That is truly how I see us as humans. If you know what you do, what you portray and if you understand the effect it has on others, you will be able to change. If you are aware of your specific behaviours that have an undesired outcome, you know what you can do to create a different effect. Recognizing the significance of various behaviours can guide you in making choices that you need to get the effect you want.

When discussing self-presentation or self-marketing, start by identifying your goal. Define exactly what you want to achieve. I've talked about defining your goal many times (see the second principle: 'Know your role, know your goal') and it's an eye-opener to start with that question if you want to enhance your self-presentation.

Your reasons for putting yourself out there can vary. You might be searching for a new job, working to promote your business or aiming to get a competitive edge in your career. When you're clear on your goals, you can better align your approach to how you want to enhance your self-presentation.

Self-marketing is putting yourself out there. It's about showing your skills, achievements and showing what makes you unique. It should not be about showing a fake persona or acting your way through life. It should not be for the outside (online) world. It should be for yourself, your presence, your goals. Your presence in your day-to-day life.

Strategy 1: Know your goal

Self-marketing should align with your goal. You might want to get noticed by your boss, but that is something completely different than your goal to stand out in a meeting to be heard (see Part Two).

For instance, if you are aiming to catch your boss's attention, you could emphasize achievements and contributions during a one-on-one. For standing out in a meeting, however, you can focus on brief and engaging communication, prepare key points and actively participate. If you focus on active effective behaviour, you will be able to use that in your work setting, during meetings, get-togethers and those all-important moments when you need to show up. It's all about impact and influence.

I once met a woman who decided to wear a red jacket to every big meeting she attended. She knew she would stand out among the crowd, where most people dressed in dark blue and grey. Her distinctive choice soon made her known as the woman in the red jacket. This recognition helped her advocate for a topic that was dear to her, as people noticed her and approached her to learn more about her mission.

Strategy 2: Analyse yourself

It's crucial to grasp that self-presentation extends beyond clothing and verbal expression – it delves into addressing behaviour and communication in various forms. And that means you have to analyse yourself. What do I do now and what is the effect I have on others? And if I want to change that effect, what should I change in my behaviour and communication? Your analysis should involve addressing various aspects of behaviour and communication. 'How do I behave myself, what do I do with my body language? How much space do I take up, how loud or soft is my voice?' This self-awareness helps you to refine your behaviour, ensuring that both verbal and nonverbal cues align with your goal and message. Seek feedback from others about your strengths and actively work on enhancing those qualities. Engaging in open and constructive conversations with peers, mentors, colleagues or even family members can provide valuable insights into your strengths, allowing you to refine and build upon them for personal and professional growth.

Strategy 3: Show yourself in your most effective way

It's essential to acknowledge that not everyone is naturally outgoing or extroverted. In these times that emphasize extroversion, individuals who identify as introverts might face challenges. So, the 'sets you apart' doesn't have to be a loud mouthing person who is wearing bright-coloured outfits. It should be behaviour that works for YOU. It should be behaviour that suits YOU – your best self and the best version of your behaviour. That doesn't mean stepping too far out of your comfort zone. It means find a way that has the effect you need by showing your qualities. For that you need authenticity: be true to yourself. Embrace your genuine interests, opinions and quirks and see how you can show them to others as well.

You have to know your strengths, accomplishments and unique qualities. Those are key to create a positive and memorable impression. It's not just about knowing them; it's about aligning this knowledge to guide your behaviour and communication. By aligning your actions and words with your goals, you can authentically express yourself, making a meaningful impact on others.

For example, I coached someone who didn't enjoy presenting. Instead of stepping on stage, he helped his team prepare for their presentations, contributing in a meaningful way without being in the spotlight himself. This approach fit with his team values, allowing him to make an impact while staying true to his preferences.

Strategy 4: Record yourself

When you want to analyse yourself and enhance yourself, make sure to record yourself on video. This creates awareness of your body language too. Reviewing these recordings can help you identify and adjust any nonverbal cues that may not be serving you well. Ensure your posture is upright, use eye contact appropriately and take up space in a way that aligns with your goals.

It's not always comfortable to watch yourself on video, but it provides invaluable feedback. Watching it with a coach can help identify specific elements of your nonverbal communication that you might not notice on your own. For instance, I once worked with a politician and we reviewed his recorded meetings to analyse his responses when speaking up. His prosody and body posture needed to be firmer and more confident. He realized the issue when he saw it, and from there, it was just a matter of training him to make the necessary adjustments.

Strategy 5: Consider the language you use

Language is an important way of expressing yourself. Ask yourself what words am I using? Is there a way you can enhance your communication? Could you upgrade your language? Clearly expressing your thoughts is very effective but make sure that you are aware of your surroundings and context. Strong language does make you stand out and gets you noticed, but it will put off others and that will never help you with your effective communication! I once coached a manager who thought harsh words and a certain language made him tough and confident. He wasn't fully aware of the extent of his language until we worked together and I brought it to his attention. After working with him he found that by cutting back on profanity and choosing his words more carefully, he noticed a more positive impact on the people around him.

Strategy 6: Consider the way you dress

Wearing an outfit that makes you feel confident can be really helpful. You might have a blouse that makes you feel extra powerful. Or some jewellery that makes you feel strong. For me, I love my heels. It's not always comfortable to wear high heels all day but I sure feel good in them. But maybe for you those amazing sneakers you got for your birthday have the same effect. The right outfit can make a big difference because it influences both how you feel and how others see you. When you feel confident in what you're wearing, that confidence naturally shows during your presentation, helping you come across as more composed and capable. Dressing thoughtfully for the occasion also signals to your audience that you've put effort into your appearance, which can boost your credibility and leave a positive impression. In the end, the right outfit supports your confidence while enhancing the impact of your presentation.

Strategy 7: Be proactive

Take the initiative by identifying opportunities for improvement and taking action on them. Proactive behaviour can set you apart. Proactive behaviour, with an eagerness to seize opportunities before they arise, makes you stand out and shows you're all about getting things done.

Express what you're working on verbally. Often, people keep their tasks to themselves, only to be surprised when they aren't approached for projects or acknowledged for their work. This failure to communicate leads to isolation in the workplace, potentially causing missed opportunities.

By verbalizing what you do and taking initiative, you not only demonstrate leadership but also show your commitment to progress and making a meaningful impact. By being proactive, you position yourself as someone who is forward-thinking, resourceful and ready to contribute to the success of both you and those around you.

I worked with a doctor in training and one of our focus areas was enhancing her proactivity. We focused on developing the habit of immediately responding when her supervisors asked a question or assigned a task. Her new approach became, 'Yes, I know the answer' or 'Yes, let me take care of that right away'.

Conclusion

Remember that being your best self is a journey and it's about discovering and embracing all those qualities that make you uniquely you. It's not about becoming someone else; it's about amplifying the best version of yourself. By understanding how you impact others and continuously refining your approach, you can build confidence, and knowing your qualities helps you to present yourself. In short, it's simple: if you know it, show it!

CHAPTER FIVE

What to do if I want to boost my confidence?

A lot of good things come from having confidence. When you feel strong and capable, you can be a force to be reckoned with, facing challenges head-on and inspiring others around you. Confidence often starts from within. It's always nice to hear feedback from others after a presentation or performance – it can be a powerful reminder of your strengths and impact. Personally, I'm grateful whenever I receive positive comments, as they can add a little extra joy after the hard work is done. For instance, when someone recently told me, 'So much of what you said resonated with how I've been thinking about our approach to difficult conversations with clients', it truly meant a lot.

However, positive feedback isn't always guaranteed, so it's essential to have ways to actively boost and maintain your confidence on your own. I once saw a video where Michelle Obama, Amal Clooney and Melinda French Gates talked about facing self-doubt (CNN, 2022). Can you imagine? It's surprising to think that even they go through it, but it's also reassuring. It reminds us that moments of uncertainty are universal and self-doubt is part of being human.

How you think about yourself, the mindset you adopt and staying consistent in building yourself up all play a role in creating lasting confidence. Trying out practical tips and making them a habit can help you feel more secure in yourself and your abilities. Here are some effective ways to build and enhance your confidence.

Strategy 1: Ask others to write something positive about you

You can ask others to write down how they perceive you. This exercise helps you gain insights into how others perceive your strengths and contributions, providing a valuable perspective that you might overlook. You can ask friends and colleagues what they like about you, what they value in your friendship or how they experience you at work.

Friends often see qualities and strengths in you that you might not recognize in yourself. By asking them to write something positive about you, you can gain a deeper understanding of the impact you have on their lives. Whether it's your ability to listen, your sense of adventure or your reliability, these positive traits can help you see yourself in a more positive light.

Colleagues can provide feedback on your professional strengths and competencies. They can highlight your skills, work ethic and contributions to the team. Understanding that your efforts are recognized and valued in the workplace can enhance your professional confidence. There are plenty of feedback forms available, but you can also come up with your own questions, such as, 'What do you enjoy most about working with me?' or 'What's the best thing I've ever done at work in your opinion?'

Strategy 2: Look back on your journey

Sometimes it's very helpful to look back and see how far I've come. Take the time to look at all the things you've done.

I enjoy reflecting on the clients I've worked with and the places I've visited. I treasure the gifts I've received from remarkable people – pens, books and even a replica of the Prague crown jewels – as reminders of the connections I've made and the experiences I've gained. Working internationally and achieving success highlight my progress and growth and looking back on past accomplishments boosts my confidence and drives me forward.

You can do the same by flipping through old files or agendas, scrolling through social media memories or browsing through photos. You might also take a moment to scan your bookshelf, remembering the books you've read or diplomas you've earned. These small acts can lift your spirits and reinforce self-worth.

If you're feeling nervous about something, like an upcoming presentation, remind yourself of similar tasks you've already accomplished. Chances are, this isn't your first time facing a challenge like this. Sometimes it helps to say out loud, 'I've done this before, so I know I can do it again.'

Strategy 3: Practise positive self-talk

We can often be our own harshest critics, saying unkind things to ourselves, but we should try to avoid talking negatively about ourselves whenever possible. When I coach others, it's disheartening to hear people genuinely calling themselves names, getting angry with themselves and thinking they are stupid or not good enough. For example, someone failed in a team meeting and called himself an 'incapable ****'. That's not the way to learn. Saying, 'I made a mistake, let me see how to learn from it and do better next time' is much more effective.

I've always struggled with the fact that I don't have a PhD. But things began to change when I fully accepted that I excel at applying science. I might not be an encyclopaedia, but I can adapt, adjust and teach others effectively. I also focus on identifying lessons and positive aspects in challenging situations. I ask myself, 'What can I learn from this and what positive outcome might arise?' Recently, someone called me the Queen of Silver Linings, a title I wear with pride. This mindset ensures that I overcome challenges and motivate others effectively. It strengthens my commitment to optimism and resilience, qualities that have been essential to my personal and professional growth. Though I sometimes still feel a bit intimidated when meeting with professors, I know my true strength lies in helping others with the practical application of all the knowledge available.

Strategy 4: Take good care of yourself

We all know how important sleep and good food are. But still. Your body, mind and soul need real care. Go to bed early, eat healthy food, go to the gym and sit on the couch. It's not always easy, especially with busy schedules and numerous responsibilities but making self-care a priority will significantly benefit your overall health and well-being. The gymnast Simone Biles is a great example of someone who understands the benefits and needs of self-care. She took a two-year break to focus on therapy and spending time with loved ones, returning to gymnastics with a renewed perspective. With rest, joy, determination and incredible skills, she is the most decorated gymnast in history.

Strategy 5: Look good and feel good

When you put effort into your appearance, it gives you an extra nudge to feel more self-assured. Investing in a pair of earrings, a shirt, a new suit or any clothing that makes you feel good can have a positive impact on your self-perception.

Wearing clothes that make you feel good about yourself is more than just a superficial act; it's about aligning your outer appearance with your inner confidence. Your appearance can influence how you perceive yourself and how others perceive you. When you dress confidently, you send a message to yourself and others that you value yourself and are ready to take on challenges.

Studies have shown that dressing well can improve your mood and increase your confidence. This phenomenon, often referred to as 'enclothed cognition', suggests that the clothes you wear can affect your psychological state and performance (Adam and Galinsky, 2012). Choosing outfits that fit well and adding accessories like a watch, necklace or a pair of stylish shoes can elevate your outfit and your confidence.

By paying attention to your wardrobe and dressing in a way that makes you feel good, you can enhance your confidence and positively influence how you interact with the world.

Strategy 6: Surround yourself with supportive people

It's important to surround yourself with positive, supportive individuals who encourage and uplift you. I once worked with a team that included one particularly negative individual, whose constant grumpiness and criticism affected everyone, including me. Nothing was ever good enough for this person; they found fault with everything and everyone and they never smiled. Such people can drain your energy, making it crucial to set boundaries to protect yourself from their negativity. It's much nicer to work with people who uplift you, make you laugh and show genuine interest in your well-being. You should address that behaviour or even make tough decisions. You might want to be transferred to a different team if people are too negative.

Strategy 7: Celebrate your successes

Acknowledge and celebrate your successes, no matter how small. It's important to create marker moments for yourself to recognize and reinforce your belief in your abilities. It's not the same as just looking back. When I achieve something remarkable, I make sure to take the time to celebrate, either by myself or with others. I often treat myself by going out to dinner or buying little gifts. I even have the gifts wrapped at the store so that unwrapping them feels like receiving a real present. Another idea is to mark achievements with a moment at the dinner table. I once worked with someone who celebrated his work success in a recommendable way: he brought home a special dessert to share with his family as a treat for a project he'd completed successfully. He briefly shared his accomplishment and his kids were so proud that they praised him and even gave him a sticker as a reward.

Conclusion

So many good things come from having confidence. When you feel strong and capable, you're unstoppable – you can take on anything, tackle challenges and even inspire others around you. Confidence gives you the push to try new things and trust that you'll figure it out, no matter what.

But remember, you don't always have to do it alone. It's important to recognize your own strengths, but if you're feeling a little shaky, don't be afraid to lean on others for a boost. Sometimes a few words of encouragement from friends, family or colleagues can remind you of just how capable you really are.

CHAPTER SIX

What to do if I want to practise new behaviour and stay true to myself?

Some people fear that they might lose their authentic selves when trying to adjust their behaviour. They believe that changing their behaviour will lead to a complete personality change and that displaying different behaviour goes against their true nature. I've encountered people who immediately claim, 'I can't do that, that's just not me!' when it comes to changing their behaviour. The belief that changing behaviour leads to a complete personality transformation and goes against one's true nature is simply not correct. Some individuals believe that their actions define their identity. They think it's impossible to show certain behaviours if those actions are not inherently part of who they are. However, a rigid mindset like that can hold you back and limit your personal growth.

Showing a specific behaviour doesn't imply a complete adoption of the personality traits others might associate with it. If you moo like a cow, you are not a cow. But if you show that behaviour in a children's play (maybe even dressed in a costume) everybody understands you are portraying a cow and that can be helpful for conveying your message.

As a director I could give an actor an instruction that is focused on the outside behaviour. I could instruct them for instance to straighten their shoulders, change their tone of voice or their proximity towards other players on the stage. This could help the audience to better understand not only the character itself, but also the character's relation towards others. These external cues assist the actor in creating a more detailed and nuanced portrayal of the character they are representing.

Alternatively, I can guide an actor to delve deeper into the internal world of their character, exploring the character's thoughts, beliefs, fears, desires and values. By helping the actor empathize with these inner qualities, I encouraged them to inhabit the character more fully from within. When an actor connects with these internal motivations, behavioural changes happen almost naturally. For example, if a character is fearful of their environment, the actor's posture may instinctively shrink, as if to avoid drawing attention or standing out. This process shows how thoughts and emotions can lead to authentic, spontaneous actions.

This dual approach – working from the outside in or the inside out – is something you can apply to our daily lives. You can adjust your behaviour by focusing on outward changes, or you can shift your mindset to bring about deeper, inner-driven changes in how you interact with the world. Both are equally valid and effective as practical paths to lasting behavioural change.

You don't have to fully change as a person; you can change your behaviour! If you want to increase your confidence, you could analyse why you're not confident, when it started and what situation, education or experience is behind it. But you could also just work on your behaviour. What can you do to show confidence? What can you adjust from the outside, even before you feel it deep inside? You can adjust your shoulders and your voice, for example.

Please know that when you haven't shown a certain behaviour in the past, it doesn't mean you are not able to show that behaviour in the future. Past results are no guarantee for the future. That's how I see behaviour. While it may seem challenging, I consistently observe that people can be influenced or nudged to adopt new behaviour. There is always an opportunity to explore new behaviour. Of course, it's nice if the new behaviour immediately aligns with you as a person, but there are many ways to challenge yourself to show new behaviour and still be the YOU you want to be.

Strategy 1: Recognize that what you do is not equivalent to who you are

By fully understanding the concept that your behaviour does not fully define you, you give yourself the freedom to experiment with your behaviour. If you do something it doesn't have to change your personality. As an example, if you are having a bad day and you are a bit snappy towards others, does that mean that you are a bad person? Does it mean that you are a bully? No, it means that on that specific day you show bad behaviour. You can apologize once you realize that. And the next day after a good night's sleep you might behave in a much gentler way. I do is not I am! The same goes for adding new behaviour to your repertoire. You can try it out and see what happens.

Strategy 2: Observe others

You can also use the approach of observing others and adapting their behaviour from the 'outside'.

You can watch the behaviour of others and copy them. For instance, if you want to seem more confident at work, you can check out someone who already looks confident (you can find tips in Chapter 16 on how to observe). You can check out what confidence looks like and study that behaviour. Perhaps there's a colleague who shows confidence in a manner you would like to adapt as well. You can mirror their body language as you would when you would 'borrow' their behaviour. If someone with confidence showcases broad shoulders, consider adopting that specific posture and observe the impact it has.

Strategy 3: Try it out before you dismiss it

New behaviour is new behaviour. It's not easy and comfortable yet. But by not giving it a chance you dismiss everything. Dismissing it without giving it a chance creates barriers before even starting. Phrases like 'I can't do that' or 'that won't work' create obstacles before you've even started. The key is to try it out first, experience its effects and then consciously decide what you want to do in the future.

In training sessions, we encourage people to practise the behaviour not only during the session but also as 'homework' in between sessions. The more data you collect on this new behaviour, the better. Interestingly, many individuals find joy in adopting the new behaviour over time. One participant even admitted, 'You were right – I just needed to try it out, and it works. I was just afraid.'

Strategy 4: Use it for a set amount of time

Adopting new behaviour doesn't have to be a permanent change, especially if it feels a bit uncomfortable. You need to step out of your comfort zone, but it doesn't have to be forever. The new behaviour doesn't have to stay with you after a time. Consider using it for a specific period. For instance, if you're in a project with a demanding leader expecting weekly client presentations and you prefer a more reserved role, assure yourself that it's okay for the time being. You can present yourself in a strong, confident way during the time of this current project. It might help you to know that it can benefit the outcome, your goals and the business. But you know it's not forever. In the next project, you can opt for a calmer role.

Strategy 5: Apply it in situations where you feel comfortable using it

Sometimes adopting a new behaviour, like saying no to your boss, may feel like a big step too soon. However, saying no to a survey on the street or over the phone could serve as an easier starting point to practice this new behaviour.

Similarly, if you're aiming to learn how to grab the attention in a meeting, which might seem challenging initially, initiating a call to the waiter in a restaurant could be a more approachable beginning. Situations may vary, but the behaviour you want to exhibit can be practised. Just try it out. Not all scenarios are the same, but the behaviour itself can be rehearsed. And as we know, practice makes perfect.

If you want to practise giving a speech, try starting at the family dinner table or during a casual get-together with friends. Want to get better at socializing at work? Attend a neighbourhood meeting to build your confidence. And if you want to work on your negotiation skills, test them out at a local market. These small, everyday moments are perfect opportunities to try out new behaviour and sharpen your skills in a relaxed setting.

Strategy 6: Make a game out of it

I recall two colleagues who needed to become more outgoing towards other divisions. They were assigned the task of communicating team updates to other teams. However, they didn't see themselves as proactive individuals and found it challenging to stand up in meetings and discuss their work. To overcome this, they introduced a small game among themselves: whoever spoke first would receive a small gift, like a coffee or a treat. This friendly competition made it enjoyable for them to step up and share, making the task much easier.

Strategy 7: Evaluate

Be sincere when evaluating your behaviour. Take time to reflect on your progress and consider how this new behaviour aligns with your values and identity. Ask yourself if it was effective, helpful and in line with what truly matters to you. Sometimes, reflecting on whether this behaviour aligns with your values can even reveal that your values have evolved over time – and that's a good thing. Adapting to new values is part of personal growth.

When you notice that this new behaviour has positive effects and brings meaningful benefits, it becomes much easier to make it a regular part of your life. Recognizing the positive outcomes helps the behaviour feel more genuine and natural, making it more 'you'. Over time, this process shapes a new version of yourself until the behaviour feels fully authentic. It might still feel a bit awkward at first, but as you start to see the positive impact, it'll keep you motivated to continue and integrate it more fully.

Conclusion

Changing behaviour does not mean changing who you are at your core. Instead, it allows you to explore different ways of interacting with the world while staying true to your values and beliefs. Behaviour can be adapted to suit different situations without altering your fundamental self. Moreover, adopting new behaviours can enhance personal growth and help you become a more versatile and confident individual, but most importantly an effective individual. It might even change how you see yourself, your values and the world.

CHAPTER SEVEN

What to do if I want to get out of my comfort zone?

Doing something you've never done before can be scary, but sometimes those intimidating tasks at work just need to be tackled, whether it's giving a presentation or attending a networking meeting (see Chapters 10 and 11). It's often about feeling scared or uncomfortable when doing something new. You don't know what might happen in an unfamiliar situation and that uncertainty can be unsettling. But sometimes we just have to step up to the plate and nudge ourselves towards challenging tasks or actions.

So, how do you nudge yourself to do something you have never done before? Or how do you overcome fears in social interaction, new tasks or embracing change?

Stepping out of your comfort zone means different things to different people. For some, it might mean approaching others in a new social setting; for others, it could be saying yes to leading their first new project. Some people are hesitant to speak up because they fear how others might interpret their words or worry that they might say the wrong thing. Others just feel overwhelmed on a day-to-day basis.

There's often a strong desire to accomplish new things and to step out of your comfort zone because you know you can benefit from it. Taking these steps is a powerful way to develop resilience and achieve personal growth. But knowing where to start can be challenging. Stepping out of your comfort zone by tackling tasks or needs step by step, even while feeling afraid, can help build confidence and gradually reduce fear.

Here are a couple of strategies to help you overcome challenges.

Strategy 1: Start where it's safe

Begin with small, manageable steps. A person I worked with aimed to become better at striking up conversations rather than avoiding social interactions. She wanted to be more spontaneous in starting conversations at gatherings and network meetings instead of hiding in a corner. She started by practising small talk in familiar settings, like meeting with a family member. She also began chatting with people on the bus and in shops, feeling that it had no lasting consequences. Gradually, she built up to more challenging situations for her, such as talking with a colleague near the coffee machine at work and eventually walking up to people and initiating conversations in a network meeting.

Strategy 2: Preparation

Preparation can help reduce anxiety by giving you a sense of control and an idea of what to expect. I once coached a man who wanted to expand his skills in unfamiliar settings. He was apprehensive about going to new places, meeting new people and exploring new work opportunities. The idea of driving to unfamiliar locations was particularly daunting for him. However, his job required him to drive more frequently and interact with others.

I gave him different assignments to prepare for his journey in advance. He started by using Google Maps to familiarize himself with the route and the area. He also visited the website of his destination to gather information about what to expect upon arrival. He chose an outfit that made him feel comfortable and professional and we prepared his speech very well. This preparation helped him feel more confident and less anxious about the trip. As a result, he was able to approach the new experience with a sense of readiness and assurance, making the unfamiliar seem more manageable and less intimidating.

Preparation can be many things: as described above, you can plan your route and research the location before driving somewhere new. Similarly, think of a few conversation starters before attending a social event. You can also use role play with a colleague to practise in advance. In a role-play session, your colleague can take on the role of someone you might meet at the event, giving you a chance to practise introductions, small talk or discussing topics you want to address. This can make you more comfortable with the kinds of responses or reactions you may receive, so you're less likely to feel caught off-guard in real situations.

Through role-play, you can also work on body language, tone of voice and pacing, which are all essential in social interactions. Practising these small details can help make your interactions feel more natural and genuine, which is key to building confidence. Additionally, feedback from a partner during role-play can be invaluable. They can let you know what feels engaging or help you adjust anything that might seem awkward or forced. By role-playing, you're essentially rehearsing and refining your social skills, helping you feel prepared and relaxed when it's time to connect in real life.

Strategy 3: Know why you are doing it

Sometimes, you simply must do what needs to be done. You might not like it, but it can be part of your job, and unless you quit, you have to step up to the plate. When you ask yourself, 'Why am I doing this?' the answer might be as simple as, 'Because I'm a professional and I have to.'

It might be helpful to reinforce your reasons: 'I'm doing this so I can pay my mortgage', 'I'm doing this to get in on that new project' or 'I'm doing this because there is nobody else who can do it'.

Of course, in the end you have a choice. If it's too scary, too uncomfortable, too tough, you might choose not to do it. It helps a lot of people to feel that most of the time they have a choice.

One person explained, 'Knowing that I have a choice helps me. When I realize I have the freedom to say no, it makes me more willing to say yes, because although it scares me, I do want to grow as a person. Knowing that I'm doing this for me, that it's my choice, helps me.'

Strategy 4: Know the positive things that might come from it

The woman who desired more interaction began engaging more after experiencing positive outcomes. She told me, 'I still don't love it, but with interaction, I always get something positive out of it, even if not all of it was positive.'

Initially hesitant and uncomfortable, she decided to step out of her comfort zone and take small steps toward increasing her social interactions. She started attending networking events, joining group discussions at work and even participating in activities after work hours.

Someone else was very happy with stepping out of his comfort zone because he felt that it enriched his life. 'I have so much more to talk about with others now and my days at work are not all the same anymore,' he said. 'It makes me feel safe that the majority of my time I have a steady workflow, but by stepping out of my comfort zone there are also special days that bring new inspiration, which is a good thing.'

Acknowledge every step you take when stepping out of your comfort zone. Embrace the effort it takes to tackle challenges and recognize the progress you're making with each attempt.

Strategy 5: Seek help in phrases and people

You might need a wing person to nudge you. This could be a colleague who asks questions to draw you into a conversation, making it easier for you to engage. Having someone by your side can create encouragement and the support that you need to step out of your comfort zone and tackle tasks that you might otherwise avoid.

For some, working with a coach or advisor can be highly beneficial. They can offer personalized guidance, helping you to develop strategies and behaviours that enhance your effectiveness. I'm honoured to continuously guide several people. Whenever they face something new, they call me and we discuss the most effective and helpful approach. One of my clients mentioned that simply knowing I'm there and that they don't have to tackle challenges alone helps them step out of their comfort zone. A coach can provide you with tools to manage your fears and gradually build your confidence in handling challenging situations.

If your fear is particularly overwhelming, it might be worth considering working with a psychologist. You might want to understand the root causes of your anxiety and develop coping mechanisms to address them. A psychologist can work with you to overcome deep-seated fears and help you build resilience, ensuring that you're better equipped to face similar challenges in the future.

You could also consider finding help in motivational quotes and phrases. In the previous chapter, you read about strategies for changing behaviour. A phrase that encapsulates this concept perfectly is Nike's 'Just do it'. This slogan nudges people not just to think about new behaviours or experiences, but to take action and actually do them. For many, it serves as a powerful motivator to overcome hesitation and step out of their comfort zones.

I also like the phrase 'Everything you want is at the other side of fear' by Jack Canfield (Canfield and Hansen, 2000). For me it means that it is okay to feel fear but that you shouldn't freeze up and become inactive. By confronting and pushing through that specific fear, you can reach your aspirations and find success. I'm glad to say it has brought me far enough to sometimes just take a deep breath and do what might be initially scary.

Jack Canfield also used the phrase, 'Don't worry about failures, worry about the chances you miss when you don't even try.' How wonderful it is to live your life to the fullest and experience those things that some others might not. What if you miss a chance? Stepping out of your comfort zone will give you experiences that you might cherish forever.

Another great example of a nudging phrase is one that is frequently (but incorrectly) attributed to fictional character Pippi Longstocking, created by writer Astrid Lindgren. She says, 'I never tried that before so I should definitely be able to do it.'

Maybe you can come up with your own catchphrase from a novel or movie that motivates you to do things. Visualizing it might help you as well. Putting it on your desktop, screensaver or phone can be a great way to remind you of action. Some people hang up posters or cards to remind them of that specific phrase that nudges them to action.

In every scenario listed here, the key is to recognize that seeking help is a strength, not a weakness. Whether it's a supportive colleague, psychologist or family member, or whether you choose to look to phrases and quotes that can push you to be the best version of yourself, these resources can significantly enhance your ability to navigate difficult tasks and improve your overall well-being.

Strategy 6: Give yourself a limited time to respond

Many people tend to overthink their actions, which prevents them from being spontaneous. So, nudging yourself with time constraints can be very effective in overcoming this. For example, I worked with a man who was afraid to speak up in meetings. To help him overcome this, we set a timer for every 15 minutes during meetings. When the timer went off, his watch would vibrate, signalling him to speak up. Even if he only said something as simple as 'I agree' or 'Does anyone want more coffee?' – or even voiced a polite disagreement – this practice helped him break through his hesitation. If he disagreed, he would express it respectfully, saying something like, 'I think I see this differently'. This approach allowed him to gradually build the confidence to participate more actively in discussions, learning to speak up regardless of whether he agreed or disagreed. Over time, these small contributions became easier and felt more natural, ultimately strengthening his ability to engage fully in conversations.

Strategy 7: Put things in perspective

Life can be challenging and certain tasks at work may feel very uncomfortable. However, it's important to put things in perspective sometimes. Feeling uncomfortable because of a presentation, for example, is temporary. Remind yourself that it's only one hour of your life and it won't define your entire career or existence. And yes, it can be intimidating to address conflicts or provide constructive feedback to a colleague. But in these moments, it's useful to remind yourself that this conversation is just a small part of your work life. Shifting your focus to the broader picture can help alleviate stress and make daunting tasks seem more manageable. Looking at the bigger picture can be really helpful. I remember a time when I didn't handle a conversation well with someone I really admire – a professor, no less. I couldn't get my question across the way I wanted and I felt a bit overwhelmed. Afterwards, I was disappointed with myself, but then I took a moment to put things into perspective. No one was hurt, it's not the end of the world and he'll likely forget it anyway, so there's no need to make a big deal out of it. We're all human, and making mistakes is part of the process.

Conclusion

Feeling uncomfortable isn't a disaster, but it's a feeling we'd rather not have. It's up to you to nudge yourself to achieve those things you set out to do and that means you must go out of your comfort zone sometimes. It takes bravery and guts but almost everyone feels happy after at least attempting those things outside of their comfort zone. Even if you don't achieve what you set out to do you can look yourself in the eye and be proud that at least you made an effort and didn't stop the process by not trying.

PART TWO

Communication

Everyone communicates constantly, all day, every day, whether it's face-to-face, on video calls or over the phone. (And while I haven't focused on written or digital communication in this book, many of the same principles still apply.)

Even choosing not to attend a meeting is a form of communication. As Paul Watzlawick taught us, 'You cannot not communicate' (Watzlawick et al, 1967). Even not showing up can signal a sense of superiority or suggest that the meeting is unimportant. Everything we do, from our behaviour and attire to our timing, words and nonverbal cues, communicates something to others. In every aspect of our daily interactions, whether intentional or not, we are constantly sending messages: through our behaviour, our choices and even our silence, reminding us that communication is inevitable and ever-present.

This part focuses on improving your communication skills, particularly in settings like meetings and presentations. It explores how to manage nonverbal struggles, such as nervous habits or distracting gestures and how to use body language effectively to reinforce the message you want to convey. It also focuses on becoming more intentional and aware of the messages you send through your behaviour.

This part of the book helps you recognize the impact of every interaction, whether it's in a meeting, a presentation or a casual conversation, giving you the tools to communicate more effectively in both professional and personal settings.

CHAPTER EIGHT

What to do if I don't know where to put my hands in a presentation?

'What should I do with my hands during a presentation?' I receive this question frequently. Those hands. They feel weird, they seem to be in the way, they almost feel like a burden sometimes.

I've seen people do all sorts of things with their hands when giving a lecture or presentation. Some clutch their notes like their lives depend on it, gripping them tightly while hardly even looking at them. They use notes as some sort of security blanket, potentially due to a lack of confidence or fear of forgetting important points. Some people grip the lectern they are in front of. They have their hands wrapped around the edges and lean on it. Or they grab the sides of it, like holding a tabletop before lifting it. Some raise their index finger and press it against the surface of the lectern with each word they speak, like pressing a key on your keyboard.

Some people play with a pen in their hands. They might click the pen, twirl it or tap it on the table without even realizing it.

This could be due to nervousness or just a need to keep their hands occupied. Even though it might seem like a small thing, it can be very distracting for both the speaker and the audience. Others try to hide their hands, maybe out of nervousness or not knowing what to do with them. It's like they're trying to keep any signs of anxiety hidden from the audience. I observed a presenter who had his hands in his trouser pockets and was fiddling with the keys hiding in there. Believe me, it was very distracting. Also holding your hands and arms behind your back is a very poor way to present.

Hiding your hands can create a sense of stiffness or rigidity, limiting natural movement and therefore connection with the audience.

Basically, not using your hands can make your presentation less effective because you don't use your body language effectively. When you limit your gestures and movements, it can be hard to show enthusiasm or make the content come alive. It might also stop you from highlighting important points, keeping the audience engaged or reacting quickly to questions and reactions. An audience likes to be engaged, and hands can help us do that.

Our hands are the go-to focus for us humans. We observe and assess hands all the time. As primates, we've consistently paid attention to the hands and mouths of others, as these were the features that could potentially hurt us. It's in our DNA to observe the hands thoroughly. So, a few strategies for what to do with them.

Strategy 1: Position your hands for immediate movement

Have the hands action ready, positioned in such a way that immediate movement is possible but not distracting. To do this, position your elbows close to your waist, letting them rest lightly against your hips or sides. Keep your hands in front of you, ready to move, almost as if you're holding a large box of chocolates with both hands, ready to offer it to someone. This 'action-ready' position makes it easier to use your hands expressively, rather than letting them hang passively at your sides.

Strategy 2: Use your hands to enhance your presentation

By positioning our hands to move, we can easily use them when we need to highlight specific elements we want to emphasize in our presentation. For instance, using your fingers to show a sum up. One, two, three. Or we can use both hands to show sizes. You can extend one hand wide apart from your body to indicate 'big', and then bring your hands close together to illustrate 'small'. Or we can use it to visualize something far away. In this case you can use your hands and arms stretched in a move to visualize the distance with your hands: 'The competition is out there'.

You can also use your hands to convey energy and enthusiasm in your presentation. For example, you might start by saying, 'This is a great day, you did so well this year', while clapping your hands together to generate excitement.

We can also use precision grips to make certain things stand out. An example of a precision grip would be the pincer grip (using the thumb and index finger to hold or manipulate small objects), but instead of holding an object you use it to show and say that something is important. It's almost like the okay sign, but the surface of the top of the thumb and index finger are flatter together and sometimes your middle finger touches the top of the thumb as well. The pinky and ring finger are usually in an upward position.

Or, you can show enthusiasm by saying, 'Let's really go for it today!' while using the following movement. Clap your hands once, hold them together for a brief moment and rub your palms back and forth slightly. This gesture is sometimes seen with salespeople who start their pitches energetically by clapping their hands or in old cartoons where characters like Scrooge McDuck are enjoying themselves.

If discussing growth, use upward hand movements; if talking about reductions, use downward gestures. This alignment helps your audience visually follow and understand your points better, making your presentation more impactful and memorable.

Strategy 3: Use congruent and effective gestures

We can use our hands effectively to show if something is significant and that we care for it. For significant points, use gestures close to your body, such as touching your chest with a flat hand when expressing sincerity or shock ('I am so honoured', 'This was shocking to me').

Make sure you always use your hands congruently and effectively. Your hand gestures should match the message you are conveying. Here's a simple example: Let's say you're talking about a big project at work. As you say, 'This project was huge for us', spread your hands wide to show how important it was. Then, if you add 'But it started with just a small idea' bring your hands or fingers close together to show the small beginning.

By matching your hand gestures to what you're saying – big gestures for big ideas and small gestures for small ones – you make your message clearer. If you say something was 'huge' but make a tiny gesture, it can confuse people and weaken your message.

Studies show that if you point right but say 'left' when giving directions, people are more likely to remember where you pointed rather than what you said. This just goes to show how strong gestures can be – they often stick more than words.

Strategy 4: Rest your hands when not emphasizing points

When you don't need to highlight or emphasize something or if you want to have a calm, poised presentation, then the advice would be: rest the hands. Keep your hands in a relaxed and still position. Rest your elbows at your waist and fold your hands together, with palms flat against each other and fingers wrapped around (but not intertwined). This posture projects calmness and composure, helping you avoid any distracting fidgeting or finger movements. Holding your hands together initially projects control and you can release them to add emphasis and movement as needed.

If you're at a lectern, you might rest your hands on it briefly but remember to avoid slouching and to use your hands as needed. I also recommend standing clear of any barriers. This helps you appear more engaged and active with your audience.

Strategy 5: Use the steeple gesture to show confidence

A steeple could work to show confidence and a good posture. In this position you place the fingertips of both hands together. The inner parts of the hand, your palms, do not touch and the fingers are spread. It's a very common display in politics: former German Chancellor Angela Merkel was famous for it. You see it in meetings and sometimes in presentations.

This is a useful way of holding your hands because it projects a sense of confidence while maintaining a professional appearance. It shows a sense of poise and control, helping you to appear composed and confident (see Chapter 5 on confidence).

Strategy 6: Slow it down

One unexpected yet effective thing you can do with your hands in a presentation is to 'freeze' mid-gesture during an important point. For example, if you're explaining a complex idea and you've used your hands to outline or emphasize it, pause for a moment with your hands in place. This stillness draws attention and makes the audience focus on what you're saying, as the lack of movement can break their expectation and signal that what you're saying is especially important.

Another unexpected approach is to use a slow, deliberate movement instead of a quick one. For instance, if you're emphasizing a big impact or a significant change, try slowly widening your arms to convey the magnitude. The slower pace builds anticipation and draws the audience's attention.

Strategy 7: Hold something

For those who are very nervous and unsure of what to do, holding an object can be a helpful strategy. By holding an object, you might feel more at ease and avoid the potential distraction of fidgeting or intertwining fingers. However, it's important to choose the right object and use it thoughtfully.

Personally, I'm not a big fan of holding papers or notes during presentations because they can become a distraction or cause you to lose connection with the audience if you look at them too often. Many people are unaware of the negative impact holding notes can have, especially when they use sloppy or dirty papers. Instead, if it's really necessary, I recommend using a small A6 card made of thick, high-quality paper. It's okay to reduce anxiety by writing down key points you need to remember, but try to do without them, if possible, to maintain a more natural and engaging presentation.

Usually I must hold a pointer for PowerPoint presentations and I hope that one day technical devices are so advanced that we can simply slightly move our finger to change slides or something similar. This would allow us to use both hands to explain things. However, that is not the case yet so if you use a pointer, don't let that arm become inactive. You can still move your arms up and down or to the side. Ensure that your body remains symmetrical. I've seen many people present with a 'dead' arm when holding the pointer, which can detract from their presentation. If you are presenting a specific object, it's often best to leave it on a pedestal first and only pick it up when necessary.

Other objects can sometimes do more harm than good. I once saw a presentation where the speaker kept glancing at his phone, which was very distracting for the audience. Instead of focusing on his message, people were drawn to his constant checking. Later, he explained that he was using his phone for notes, but to me, it looked unprofessional. It can make a speaker seem unprepared or uninterested, even if that's not the intention. Rather than enhancing the presentation, the phone became a distraction, reducing both the professionalism and impact of his message.

Conclusion

Using hand gestures in a presentation makes it clearer and more engaging. With all of this in mind, the key factor when you're using your hands is maintaining variety and clarity. Holding onto a single gesture or posture without any changes can become both distracting and boring. Remember, our brain likes novelty and it's hardwired to register what people do with their hands, so using your hands in many various ways will help you to clarify content in your presentation, and it will also keep your audience entertained and engaged. Be conscious of how you use objects; it can reduce nervousness during your presentation but make sure it looks professional.

CHAPTER NINE

What to do if I have to prepare for a presentation?

You are drinking your coffee, going through emails and all of a sudden you see your colleague at the door of your office: 'Come quickly, John is sick. Please can you fill in the client on the latest status of the project?'

Your heart skips a beat. An unexpected presentation! We've all had that moment in life when we had to present without being able to prepare fully. Maybe it was because you completely forgot it was your turn to present the numbers in the meeting or maybe it was because you had to fill in on the spot. The result is the same for most people. Your heart is racing and your breathing is high up in your chest.

In situations like these, stress is usually the main problem, so it's important to keep yourself calm and collected. There are many ways to reduce this stress. If you're wondering how to calm your nerves, check out Chapter 10 in this book.

But the answer in this chapter here will focus on a plan. Because when you know what to do to create a good presentation and focus on both the content and delivery, your confidence will increase, allowing you to give a speech with assurance. With structure you can deliver information in a clear, logical and engaging manner, whether you have 10 minutes, 10 days or 10 months to prepare.

Giving a presentation is actually not that hard at all if you keep three essential things in mind: first, understand your audience. Second, know your message. And third, be aware of the time – in other words, the WHO, WHAT and HOW LONG. Even if you have only a short amount of time to prepare you can give a great presentation.

This happened to me during a seminar when one of the speakers suddenly fell ill. The organizers approached me and asked if I could step in and give a presentation about behaviour on the spot. The presentation was only 35 minutes long, but without any visuals like PowerPoint or thorough preparation, it might feel different and challenging. However, I used the following to create a great presentation on the spot. Here's what helps.

Strategy 1: Know your audience

Before you start presenting, know who you are presenting for. Is it a client? Your colleagues? Understanding your audience's background and level of familiarity with the topic is crucial for effective communication. I once taught a session on nonverbal communication specifically for a group of five-year-old toddlers. This audience differs from the board of the medical company I recently presented to on the same subject. I must say, I really enjoyed how those toddlers had more energy in their pinkies than the entire boardroom combined.

Before you begin to share, make sure you know who is there!

Also, during your presentation, be prepared to adapt based on the cues you receive from your audience. If you notice that certain concepts are unclear or too advanced for them, be ready to simplify or provide additional explanations. Keeping things simple is effective because if our words are too complex, it can distract others and stop them from understanding the content.

Keeping things simple works best because if your language is too complicated, it can distract people and make it harder for them to follow along. If you keep it simple you focus on conveying your message in a way that is accessible to everyone, regardless of their level of expertise or familiarity with the topic.

Also, keep in mind that not everyone will know the same abbreviations or terms you do. Being aware of who you're talking to helps you out when you move to Strategy 2, where the focus is on *what* you're actually saying.

Strategy 2: Know the what

What should I present and how should I structure my presentation?

When considering what you want to say, start by writing down one sentence capturing the essence of your presentation. That sentence should contain what you want your audience to know. The take-away, so to speak. It could be the message you want them to take back to their colleagues or the essential action they need to implement. For example: 'After this presentation I want people to understand that our budget is fine for now, but I also want to emphasize the importance of closely monitoring it.' Or 'After this presentation, I want the team to know that our main focus is improving customer satisfaction and everyone should prioritize quick response times.'

Once you have the essence of your presentation summarized in one sentence, the next step is to identify three or four key words or phrases that you want to include in your talk. These words could represent crucial percentages that you need to convey or the remaining budget. Alternatively, they could be difficult or technical terms that you want to make sure you remember to use effectively during your presentation.

For example, if you are presenting a marketing report, your one-sentence essence could be: 'I want my audience to know that our campaign succeeded because we boosted brand awareness by 15 per cent. Now, during the last quarter, we must be smart about budgeting for long-term growth.'

The key words might include 'campaign performance', 'customer engagement' and 'market trends'.

Having these key words noted down can serve as reminders during your presentation, helping you stay on track and ensuring that you cover the important points you want to convey. It also provides a safety net for remembering difficult terms or figures that might be crucial to your talk.

Give yourself a sentence to start with to make it easier for yourself: 'Dear all, thank you so much for being here to hear about the latest results on our marketing campaign.' A starting sentence can help ease you into the presentation and set a positive tone. It also acknowledges the audience's presence and appreciation for their time.

If you don't have the time to write all of this down, just structure it in your head and reduce your words to three important ones you will remember. Saying them out loud while walking to the presentation room might help you as well.

Strategy 3: How long

The pace and speed of your presentation plays an important role in delivering your message effectively. Starting strong and maintaining a good pace throughout will ensure that your audience receives the information you intended to convey within the given time. If you have only 10 minutes to present a topic and you start slow, your time management might fail and therefore your message.

If you struggle with time management, there are simple ways to stay on track. You can keep an eye on the clock or ask someone to assist you by indicating the remaining minutes using their fingers or writing the time left on a piece of paper.

When preparing your presentation, it's helpful to split it into three main parts: Start, Middle and End. Write down how much time you plan to spend on each section. However, instead of just three parts, consider focusing on five phases: Introduction, Start, Middle, End and After Moment. Include an Introduction if the audience doesn't know you and don't forget the After Moment, where you stay engaged and prepared to answer questions even after your presentation is over.

Strategy 4: Introduce yourself and the topic

When presenting to an audience that doesn't know you, it's important to introduce yourself. In some settings, someone else may introduce you, but that might not always be the case, especially in meetings. Additionally, introduce the subject you will discuss. Starting with an 'attention grabber' can be effective. This could be an anecdote, similar to what you see in TED Talks. If you don't have time to craft an applicable story, simply engaging the audience by making eye contact, stating your name and clearly presenting your topic is a good way to begin your presentation. 'My name is Anne-Maartje Oud and I'm a behavioural expert. I'd like you to think about a conversation you've had that you consider to be bad. Today, I'm here to share some tips on how to improve those difficult conversations and how to make them more effective.'

Strategy 5: Start smart and engaging

This is where you deliver your core message you wrote down. You can say it very clearly: 'After this presentation I would like you to go to your colleagues and thank them because our brand campaign succeeded.' But you can also ask a question to grab your audience's attention. 'What would you do to save money on our budget? We need to make sure that happens in the future!' Make certain to deliver the core message early in your presentation. Because when time flies and suddenly you have no more time left while you are presenting, you've at least given them the message they need to absorb.

Strategy 6: Have an informative middle

The middle section is the core of your presentation, where you share the main ideas and provide the depth your audience needs. Depending on the time you have, the middle of your presentation can either offer a quick overview or dive deeply into the topic. This is your chance to offer real value – whether that's giving an overview or going in-depth on key points. A strong, informative middle keeps your audience interested and helps them connect with the material.

If you enjoy speaking and have plenty of time, feel free to fill this part with lots of material – elaborate, give examples, share stories and detailed insights to keep your audience engaged.

If you're running short on material or drawing a blank, turn to the audience for input. Engage them by asking questions related to the topic, like, 'Since you've been part of the project, how do you feel about our progress?' This not only involves them but taps into the valuable insights they bring.

Your audience likely has good ideas and perspectives worth sharing. Ask how they view the topic or how they would define it. This interaction creates a lively atmosphere and encourages them to bring up important questions they might otherwise hold back. In this way, you're not just delivering information – you're creating a conversation.

Strategy 7: Conclude effectively and maintain presence

Conclude your presentation by summarizing your key points and repeating the most important message. By rounding up your presentation it's important to leave them with the essence of the takeaway message. What do you want them to remember? But simply repeating your key message you started with is also possible. Summarize what you've said and repeat the most important message: 'This project is going great because all percentages are met; now we have to budget smart for the future!' Use quotes or concise statements to leave a lasting impression.

The last focus is the After Moment. After finishing a presentation, some people become so excited and are so relieved that they forget they are still on stage or in the conference room. It's important to understand that you are still in your role and your message is lingering, so you still need to be alert. Please leave the stage with dignity and a calm body language. Additionally, you should be prepared to answer any questions they might have during coffee breaks or networking events after the presentation. Remember: 'A presentation is only done when everybody is gone!'

Conclusion

Presenting on the spot can be challenging, but a clear structure can make all the difference. It acts as a guide, helping your presentation flow smoothly and making the experience more manageable and impactful. Focus on the Who, Why and What to stay on track and remember to engage your audience by asking questions to encourage participation and make it more interactive.

If you can't prepare for a meeting, practise what you would say in one minute, identify the main takeaways with a few words and jot down the essential points. This helps you stay focused and ensures you deliver key information effectively, even without extensive preparation.

CHAPTER TEN

What to do if I'm nervous about a presentation?

It's completely normal to feel nervous, even if you've done countless presentations before. Singer Adele has been honest about her fear before a performance. Before coming on the stage she struggles with anxiety, up to the point where she sometimes needs to vomit.

Her audiences might be different than the one you face. And the numbers of her audience might differ as well. But here's the thing, whether you're presenting to a small group of five or a massive audience of 50,000, your body doesn't really care about the difference. When you are nervous, you are nervous. The thought of standing in front of a group of people and being the centre of attention can be nerve-wracking for some people (but not for all, of course).

Unfortunately, being nervous doesn't help us to present and perform the way we want to. And being nervous doesn't help us to be effective. Our throat dries up, our breath is high up our chest, we might even feel we are going to faint. When we experience high levels of stress, our limbic system 'takes over' our rational thinking and cognitive abilities. We can't think clearly anymore. Our cognitive brain can't work as effectively as we want it to, making it difficult to think clearly and logically. It's harder to organize our thoughts, we have difficulty recalling information and our focus seems almost out of the window. But during a presentation, that is just what we need: focus.

I once coached someone who needed help. He quit his previous job because he feared giving presentations. He didn't want to go through the stress of presenting anymore, so he left that job. Avoiding presentations might seem like an easy way to deal with the stress, but in the end, it can hold you back from moving forward in your career and getting better opportunities. Giving presentations is a smart choice because it enhances your communication skills, builds your confidence, opens doors for networking and can elevate your career while allowing you to share your ideas and leave a meaningful impact on others. Anxiety about presenting can affect your career and personal growth. Once this person started his new job, he found out that he still had to do presentations and it made him realize that he needed some support to feel less nervous. That's when he made the decision to get coaching to help him overcome his fear.

The best way to handle pre-presentation jitters is to minimize stress before and during your presentation. This helps you present yourself and your content effectively to achieve your goals. So, how can you do that?

Strategy 1: Know your content

First, knowing your content is helpful. Having a clear idea of what you want to say and preparing your presentation in advance is a smart way to ensure that you convey your message effectively. You can create a PowerPoint for structure, make notes, write cue cards; all things to help you with a reference and anchor during your presentation. Beforehand you can rehearse by yourself, out loud in your car or in front of a mirror, or you can rehearse in front of friends and colleagues. Sometimes I recommend people record themselves on video so that they can watch it back and observe their own behaviour and listen to what they say. It helps you identify areas to improve. Doing this regularly and practising your content can reduce stress and improve your performance.

But even when you know every word by heart, you still might feel nervous. You can't sleep the days before, you think of what might go wrong, the unexpected questions you might get or how the audience will react. It could be a fear of judgement from the spectators, a pressure to perform perfectly or a lack of confidence and fear of failure. In essence: you are stressed. So, what to do with that?

Strategy 2: Realize stress is normal

By validating your feelings and turmoil thoughts and recognizing this is not unique, you will naturally calm yourself and come to understand that feeling nervous before a presentation is normal for many people. Knowing this helps you see that it's okay to feel nervous and it encourages you to use strategies to manage those feelings and improve your performance.

For example, before a big presentation, take a moment to remind yourself, 'Feeling nervous is just part of the process and it happens to everyone'. This mindset allows you to shift your focus from worry to preparation, empowering you to apply relaxation techniques that will help you feel more in control and confident on stage.

Strategy 3: Mind your breathing

Breathing is very effective. A deliberate cathartic exhale (the one we automatically use after dodging an intense situation) could help us. You take a deep breath in and with breathing out you puff your cheeks and let the air flow out, blowing out so you feel the air flowing over your lips. Almost like a whistle. Taking intentional deep breaths and using a relaxed breathing pattern can be really helpful in calming the body's natural reaction to stressful situations. When we practise controlled breathing, it has been found to have positive effects on our physical well-being, such as lowering blood pressure and our heart rate. With that we can reduce the levels of stress hormones.

Strategy 4: Use your body

Using your body to distract you from your thoughts by actively engaging in an activity can help you. I like to jump up and down like an athlete getting ready for a race, getting the blood flowing and stretching the muscles. Other techniques are pushing your hands against a wall (as if you are the big bad wolf not only huffing and puffing with your breathing but also pushing the wall away). These techniques help to release tension in the body, easing stress and promoting a sense of calm.

For some people this has the opposite effect. They get even more nervous when they get the blood flowing. For them a more meditative approach could be effective.

Strategy 5: Meditative approach

One other technique I like to use is having a coffee, closing my eyes and trying not to get distracted by everyone around me. Just me, myself and I. Focusing on what is about to come. Also, the warm beverage in your hand will calm you down. We have a lot of nerves in our hands and fingers and holding a cup of as well as drinking tea has been known to help people reduce stress. Another technique is sucking on a candy or chewing gum, which can help keep your mouth moist and reduce any feelings of dryness before a presentation. This makes sense as it's a pacifying behaviour and we need a way to calm our nervous system. Make sure you take it out during your presentation. You can also stare out of a window, listen to some music or even try an online meditation. Focus on your breathing, or you might want to put on some calming sounds. Instead of getting caught up in negative thoughts or letting fear take over, try to concentrate on the present moment and stay calm and focused right now.

Strategy 6: Be in the moment

During a presentation it's key to be in the moment and to not get carried away by the things you might say or forget to say. You are the only one who knows the content of your presentation, so if you happen to leave something out, don't make it a big issue. Ed Miliband, former leader of the UK Labour Party, once gave an hour-long party conference speech without notes. Even though he later admitted he forgot some information, he defended his approach, saying he had communicated honestly and directly with his audience, which was more important than the content of his speech. Additionally, don't worry about getting distracted by looking at your audience. They might seem busy with their phones, which could be perceived as a distraction, but they could actually be taking notes. Remember to maintain a calm, low voice and keep taking deep breaths as you speak. Holding your notes might help you, as well as a pen to prevent yourself from fidgeting. Make sure your body language is active. Using the Power Pose, perfectly explained by Amy

Cuddy in her famous TED Talk, might help you to feel confident and strong. You use your body by adopting a confident, expansive posture (like standing tall with hands on hips). It's a pose that noticeably gives people confidence. You can use it to prepare beforehand, but you can also use it during the presentation to let this posture have a positive effect on your confidence and reduce stress. Also, a glass of water to clear your throat can be helpful.

Strategy 7: Talk about it with others

If you keep your worries to yourself, you might end up feeling even more anxious. Talking about your feelings with colleagues or friends can give you a new perspective. For example, I once had a big presentation coming up and I was dealing with the nerves on my own. But when I opened up to a friend, his caring response really helped. He understood what I was going through, shared his own similar experiences and we exchanged stories about how we'd handled nervousness in the past. Just getting it out there made a big difference. Sharing really is caring, isn't it?

Conclusion

In essence, there are many things to choose from when it comes to calming yourself down. There are plenty of things you can try. Find what works best for you and what helps you feel relaxed. You can distract yourself by having a chat with someone, cracking jokes or talking about something unrelated. The important thing is to discover what brings you peace and helps you relax. By using that in your routine before and during a presentation, you'll feel more confident, focused and ready to perform at your best. When you prepare your content and rehearse, you'll have the confidence to speak clearly and effectively. Additionally, mind your breathing and focus on the present moment. Lastly, remember to relax your body – tension can hinder your delivery, so staying loose and at ease will help you engage your audience more naturally.

CHAPTER ELEVEN

What to do if I need to attend a networking meeting?

Not everyone's into networking. For some, grabbing a drink post-work or following a seminar feels like a good time, but it's interesting how many people bring up their networking fears and apprehension during coaching sessions. They're looking for tips on navigating networking events. 'What should I talk about? How do I avoid being awkward?' The thought of starting conversations with strangers or making connections with potential prospects can be pretty overwhelming for many. Questions like 'What's the right thing to say?' or 'How can I leave a good impression without looking like I'm overdoing it?' are all too common.

Networking is more than just socializing; it's about creating genuine connections in a way that's comfortable and authentic, but still with a possible outcome for your business goals. It can also be that drink after work or attending the office Christmas party. This doesn't come naturally to everyone, though.

It's important to know that networking meetings are common and important and it's good to know what you can do to help yourself and your company to make your visit successful.

Strategy 1: Prepare

Make sure you know what meeting you are going to and prepare accordingly. Take the time to thoroughly read the invitation or event details. Familiarize yourself with the venue, what's expected of you, the schedule, the attire and who will be in attendance. Although it may appear trivial, many situations arise where attendees arrive late and flustered because they were unaware of logistical details such as parking arrangements.

Dress appropriately for the event's setting to make a good first impression. On one occasion, I was invited to an exclusive event at the Rijksmuseum in Amsterdam, which included a walking dinner and an award ceremony. Guests were explicitly requested to dress formally. Unfortunately, a few attendees stood out uncomfortably, wearing jeans and sweaters amidst a sea of black-tie attire. That's not how you want to start your meeting.

Also remember to bring essential materials like business cards, a QR code or a notepad and a pen for exchanging contact information and jotting down important points during or shortly after your conversations. While you can easily use your phone for these tasks, keep in mind that in some settings or cultures, it might be seen as rude or distracting to rely on your phone instead of more traditional methods.

Strategy 2: Know why you are there

Before attending a networking meeting, it's crucial to understand your objectives. Set clear and achievable goals before the meeting, such as meeting five new people or getting feedback on a specific topic. Prepare a concise and compelling elevator pitch that covers who you are, what you do and what you are looking to achieve.

Knowing why you are there will help you focus your efforts and make the most out of the event. Are you aiming to make a new connection, gather insights on others' reactions to the presentation beforehand, reconnect with a long-lost client or simply enjoy yourself? There are lots of options to consider and to prepare for.

Consider if your goal is to make new connections. If so, prepare a brief introduction about yourself and your work. That short elevator pitch is helpful to communicate who you are, what you do and your proposition. Think about how you can add value to others and what you can offer in terms of knowledge or resources.

If you aim to gather insights on others' reactions to a presentation or project, come prepared with specific questions to ask attendees.

When reconnecting with a long-lost client, do some research on their recent activities or achievements. With that information you can start a meaningful conversation and show that you have taken an interest in their work. Mention specific past interactions to reignite the connection and discuss potential opportunities for collaboration.

Sometimes, networking meetings are simply about enjoying yourself and building rapport in a relaxed setting. In this case, focus on being approachable and friendly. Engage in lighthearted conversations, share stories and participate in any social activities planned for the event.

Strategy 3: Talk to the right people

Consider who will be in at the network meeting and if there's anyone specific you want to meet. You can do this in advance. Many seminars offer a list of attendees in advance, allowing you to research individuals online. Additionally, LinkedIn and other social media platforms are useful for identifying who might announce their attendance at an event. Additionally, during the event, if you see someone you'd like to meet, you can ask others to introduce you or you can take the initiative to approach them yourself. When doing so, do it in a friendly and approachable way, rather than being overly direct. Don't be blunt, be amiable.

Strategy 4: Dare to interrupt

Easing into a conversation during a networking event is an art. To slide into a conversation at a networking event without coming off as rude is all about timing and approach. First you need to wait for a natural break in the conversation. Jumping in mid-sentence is not advised. It's about finding that pause where you can smoothly enter without causing a ripple. As you spot your moment, catch the eye of someone in the group and offer a friendly smile, it's almost a silent, 'Hey, mind if I join?' Then, with a polite 'Excuse me' or 'May I join you?' you gently make your intentions known. This approach could also be verbal, enriching the conversation and leaving a positive mark. For example, you might say, 'I recently read an article on this topic' and then share an interesting fact to enrich the discussion.

Of course, always read the room, if the conversation seems intensely private or the group is deeply engrossed, it might be better to find a different opening. This way, you navigate the networking seas with finesse, making connections smoothly and respectfully.

Strategy 5: Go with a colleague

The thought of attending an event alone can trigger anxiety for some people. If the idea of going solo to a networking event fills you with dread, consider bringing a colleague along. When doing this, it's important not to fall into the trap of spending the entire event in your comfort zone, simply chatting with your colleague and excluding others. While bringing a familiar face can ease your initial fears and provide moral support, the goal is to use this as a stepping stone. Encourage each other to branch out and connect with new people. Set a goal, like 30 minutes, and then meet back up with your colleague to share experiences. This approach can help you navigate the networking scene more comfortably, allowing you to slowly but surely extend your professional circle while still having a safety net to return to when needed.

Strategy 6: Create conversation starters

For some, social anxiety poses a real challenge, making it hard to start or join conversations with new people.

However, using specific conversation starters can ease the process of engaging. Personally, interacting comes easily to me. I have a genuine love for meeting new people and a curiosity about their reasons for attending and their personal or business stories. Everything can be a conversation starter, from the flowers in the room to mentioning the logo on someone's badge.

Consider asking about their impressions of the speaker, whether they've attended a similar seminar before or, if you're at the buffet, their thoughts on the food, drinks or overall organization. Questions like 'What prompted you to sign up for this?' or 'What's been the highlight of the seminar for you?' can open the door to engaging exchanges.

Strategy 7: Body language

When seeking interaction with others, it's essential to observe their body language (Chapter 16). You should observe well as you may not always want to interrupt or start a conversation. If you see them close to each other, whispering, almost like gossiping, you might not want to interrupt that conversation. However, most of the people at networking meetings know that they are there to connect and interact and therefore will mostly be open to talk.

Adopting an open and active posture will create a different response compared to turning away from others or hiding in a corner, hoping someone will approach you.

By positioning yourself near a group, you're likely to be noticed and someone may take the initiative to include you in the conversation. Pay attention to their eye contact, positioning yourself in the view of the person leading the discussion so they might pick up on you and invite you to join. Look people in the eye and have an active posture. Displaying openness and readiness for conversation is key. Stand with your shoulders back, chest forward and show confidence by maintaining eye contact without hesitation. Use your smile and nod your head to engage with others. Recently, at a networking event, someone quickly noticed that I wanted to join their conversation – they were very observant. I encourage everyone to be mindful of body language and to make an effort to include others who show interest in joining the discussion.

Conclusion

In conclusion, when networking, remember to be prepared, observe body language cues, adopt an open and active posture and position yourself strategically near groups for potential inclusion in conversations. And don't forget to have fun. After all, networking is not just about professional advancement but also about building meaningful moments and enjoying the process. Humans are both interesting and intriguing so enjoy the connection! Keep in mind that the best connections often happen when you're genuine, approachable and truly present in the moment.

CHAPTER TWELVE

What to do if I am looking for the most significant nonverbal cues?

There are over 4,000 nonverbal cues registered; if you want to study them all you must work hard. But what if you want to focus on the main cues that could benefit you in your work situation?

By observing your colleagues when communicating it might be too much to take in all their body language all at once. But if you train yourself by focusing on some specific, important cues it will get you far. I've chosen seven cues for you to observe during your conversations with people.

The most important focus point you will ever observe is spotting comfort or discomfort when it comes to nonverbal communication. Do I see comfort or do I see discomfort? This in itself can already give you so much information about your conversational partner. Do they feel at ease or not? Are they relaxed or tensed? Are they showing that they want to communicate or do we see them distancing themselves from us?

By identifying the basis of comfort and discomfort during communicating you can understand if you are on the right track with your conversation. If you see discomfort, it might be a sign of not being on the right track. It gives you an indication that you might have to change your behaviour to create a better and more effective conversation. Always be very mindful that we have to take context into consideration; not every gesture is a message waiting to be decoded.

So many writers and researchers have shaped our understanding of nonverbal communication: Desmond Morris, Joe Navarro, Paul Ekman, Albert Mehrabian, Bella DePaulo, David Matsumoto, Amy Cuddy, etc. I highly recommend delving into all their books to gain a deeper understanding. However, for this chapter I focused on the seven behaviours that serve as intriguing indicators during conversations.

So, what can we look for?

To learn how to observe effectively, read Chapter 16 of this book. Once you've done that, you can begin applying your observation skills. The following body language behaviours will be a helpful starting point.

Strategy 1: Furrowed glabella

The glabella is the area between the eyes and just above the nose. In my opinion, it's one of the most straightforward signals someone can send during a conversation to indicate that something might be bothering them. This becomes particularly relevant when you're in a negotiation or a challenging discussion, as a furrowed glabella can strongly suggest disagreement with what you're saying or express doubts about the topic being discussed.

Strategy 2: Hands-on-hands touching

The behaviour of pacifying hands-on-hands involves actions like handwringing, stroking the hands, touching the fingers and intertwining the fingers. These gestures are usually indicative of someone trying to comfort or soothe themselves. These self-soothing actions may serve as a physical expression of emotional discomfort or an instinctive response to bring a sense of calmness during challenging or uneasy situations. We call them pacifying behaviours and they can show discomfort very quickly.

Strategy 3: Touching of face and neck

Pacifying behaviour on a face involves actions such as touching your face, stroking your forehead with one or two hands or plucking your face with your fingers, touching or stroking the neck. We should also observe the pressure that is used for the massaging and stroking. The more pressure, the more stress, you could say. We've all seen the pictures of businessman losing a lot of money and stroking their forehead and neck. These moves usually suggest someone might be feeling uneasy or uncomfortable. When someone shows this behaviour, it might be because they want to self-soothe or ease stress.

Strategy 4: Pacifying behaviour with objects

When people touch objects like pens, a mug they are holding or start fidgeting with the papers in front of them, we might see a sign of discomfort or even nervousness. When people feel uneasy or apprehensive in a situation, they may instinctively seek comfort or relief by interacting with nearby objects.

For example, someone might twirl a pen in their hand during a tense meeting or repeatedly adjust the position of a mug on the table while discussing a challenging topic.

Recognizing these cues allows us to respond with empathy and understanding, creating a supportive environment that encourages comfort and openness.

Strategy 5: Ventral denial

When we are having a conversation with someone and they turn their body away from us, this might be an indication of not being fully engaged in the conversation or it might be trying to create some emotional distance. This behaviour can be a response to feeling threatened, uneasy or wanting to avoid a topic of discussion. In some cases, it could also be a subconscious attempt to establish personal space or boundaries.

Strategy 6: Lips disappearing or lip biting

Joe Navarro (2018) summarizes this behaviour with the following sentence: 'When the lips disappear, trouble is near.' Of course, we have to consider the context with all the behaviours discussed in this chapter. It's not always 100 per cent certain that it is an indication of trouble, but when people suck in their lips, bite their lips or press really hard on their lips this can be a clear indication of stress.

Our lips, filled with nerve endings, are very sensitive to what's happening around us. When we're under stress, like hearing bad news, our lips often respond by becoming thinner or pressing tightly together – and in moments of intense stress, they can even seem to disappear completely. I've noticed this in public many times, and I sometimes check in with people to see if they're okay. This small gesture has led to meaningful conversations, where people feel comfortable getting things off their chest. One woman even thanked me afterwards, saying, 'Thank you for asking if something was wrong – you reminded me I'm not alone.'

Strategy 7: Cathartic exhale

You observe puffing up the cheeks and then a deep exhale with the lips pursed as if someone is whistling but with hardly any sound. It's like blowing out a candle but with more air in the cheeks. It's a visual sign that shows how someone's feeling, especially when they're relieved or stressed. Additionally, you might notice raised eyebrows and wider eyes during these moments.

Conclusion

By actively observing these nonverbal signals, you not only gain a deeper understanding of others, but you also have the opportunity to adapt your own behaviour to better connect with others and support them. It can significantly enhance our ability to interact effectively and create positive relationships with those around us. After all, according to me, 'One of the keys to effective communication is observation!'

CHAPTER THIRTEEN

What to do if I want to have effective conversations?

From my experience working in different organizations and chatting with many professionals, one thing stands out: people should focus on mastering the art of effective conversations. There is so much miscommunication in companies and unfortunately, effective communication skills are rarely taught in schools. It's not that we don't know how to converse, but often we are not taught about the subtle ways of interaction.

Effective conversations aren't just about time management and clear communication. They're also about mastering interaction skills, whether it's in a planned or unexpected meeting. It's about using the so-called 'soft skills' such as active listening, summarizing and showing empathy. By applying all these skills professionals can contribute to much smoother communication and better overall team performance and collaboration.

When I work with organizations on basic communication skills like listening and speaking, I'm always amazed by how grateful people are when they receive the tools and personal feedback to improve. They often share feedback later, expressing their surprise at how tweaking these essential skills has significantly benefited their workplace interactions. So, what can you do to make things better?

Strategy 1: Prepare

Certainly, the content of what you're going to say is important, but it's not just about preparing the words you will use. Think about the whole scene – where are you chatting about, what is the location, what time of day is it? What is your aim for this conversation? How much time do you need?

Make sure you know what you want to get out of the conversation and adjust how you approach it. Also, it's important to know who's going to be there. How many people will attend? Do you have to address a group of people or is it just one colleague? Think about who's coming and what they might be looking for. What might be their goal in the conversation?

Strategy 2: Know your role, know your goal

One of my key teachings is 'Know your role, know your goal'. Defining your role is crucial because, for example, giving advice as a friend is entirely different from giving advice as a manager. The goal of the conversation is equally important: what needs to be achieved at the end of the conversation? These are all things to consider in your preparation. You're doing more than just planning what to say; you're setting everything up for a meaningful and effective conversation. And consider if it's your role to engage in that specific conversation in the first place.

A conversation might follow a structured meeting format, but it can also pop up unexpectedly and catch you off guard.

For example, someone might ask you about a project while you're grabbing coffee. In these unplanned moments, it's still important to use your communication skills effectively. Even if you haven't prepared, you can still have a goal in mind or quickly get a sense of the other person's intentions.

If the conversation was planned, it's a good idea to share your goals or ask about theirs ahead of time. For spontaneous talks, you can ask about their intentions on the spot. Use your soft skills to keep the discussion productive and meaningful. You might even ask directly, 'Could you please let me know what you consider to be the goal here?' And don't forget to consider if it's truly your role to engage in that particular conversation. If not, it might be more effective to connect them with the right person.

Strategy 3: Listen

I love this quote from Epictetus: 'We have two ears and one mouth so that we can listen twice as much as we speak.' However, putting it into practice is easier said than done! Most of us love to chat, explain things or share our knowledge. But when it comes to having meaningful conversations, sometimes we've just got to be silent and listen. We need to pay close attention to the words being used. It's like putting the conversation under a microscope: observing the specific words chosen, the order in which they're delivered, listening for any repetition and listen whether certain words are emphasized. Listening sounds simple, but often we cut conversations short, jump in too soon or turn them into monologues. In the Netherlands, a dating show drew a lot of negative reactions when it revealed how frequently people go through first, second and even third dates without asking a single question – just talking nonstop. Sadly, I see this happen in business too.

Turn-yielding is essential. Sometimes you talk, sometimes someone else talks. So, let's make an effort and zip it!

Strategy 4: Summarize

When you are listening, note or write down main ideas or specific details that seem important. If it's not possible to write them down do this in your head. After that you can reflect back. Use phrases like 'What I'm hearing is...', 'So, you're saying that...' or 'It sounds like...' to repeat back the essence of what the other person has communicated. If you're unsure about something, you can check by asking clarifying questions. For example, 'Did I get that right?' or 'Is this what you mean?' Your summary should be short and focused, the core message of the other person without adding your own interpretation or opinion. It not only demonstrates active listening but can also clarify misunderstandings before they escalate. Make sure that the other person is heard.

Strategy 5: Ask questions

I mentored a doctor who was learning to effectively communicate with patients. To improve his skills, we conducted practice sessions with actors, focusing on how to encourage patients to change their behaviour. Initially, he tended to push his ideas onto patients, which is often met with resistance. We worked on refining his approach to include asking open-ended questions – such as 'who', 'why', 'what' and 'when' – to foster a more open and receptive dialogue (who can help you, what do you need, what do you understand so far, what can I make clear, why are you reluctant to change your behaviour, etc?). He then applied these techniques in real-life scenarios. To the delight and surprise of the doctor, the patient praised him for asking questions and being thorough in his approach. This led to a moment of realization for the patient, who acknowledged that their behaviour was negatively impacting their health. Also, the doctor had a moment of realization: by asking questions you can achieve a great result.

Strategy 6: Focus and observe

It's easy to get distracted. Sometimes we steer away from the content and goal that was set in the beginning. I always advise people to write down in one sentence what they want to discuss beforehand. This allows for easy reference during the conversation, helping to maintain focus. With a clear focus, you can steer the discussion back to its main objective if it starts to wander. For example, if the conversation shifts from project deadlines to brainstorming new product ideas, you'll know you're off course and need to guide it back.

Also think about external factors that can disrupt the conversation. This could be anything from movements outside glass windows, background chatter in an open office setting or background music. A lot of things can be quite distracting. Too many people stare at their phones during conversations; this sadly prevents a lot of people from observing what is going on during the conversation.

Strategy 7: Follow up

At the end of the conversation, assess if you've achieved your initial goal. If you did, it likely indicates that you had an effective conversation. But remember that the effectiveness of a conversation isn't just about what happens during the talk but also about what follows. A common pitfall is failing in the follow-up. If you've made any promises, ensure you deliver on them. Do you need to take action, email someone or inform others about the conversation? Try to do this directly afterwards. Often, daily tasks distract us, especially after a spontaneous conversation at the coffee machine. Although unscheduled, such meetings can generate tasks that require follow-up. It's important to take action and not to forget about them. If you deliver on your promises, you enhance your trustworthiness and pave the way for more effective future conversations.

Conclusion

Conversations happen constantly, but they're not always as effective as they could be. To make the most of them, start by knowing what you want to achieve and commit to improving your skills. Observe, be focused and engaged. Practise as much as you can, reflect on every conversation and you'll see how every conversation will enhance your skills.

CHAPTER FOURTEEN

What to do if I want to become better at online meetings?

Remote work is here to stay and many companies now have more online meetings than in-person ones. It's up to us to train ourselves and our teams to become better at this format. And although this chapter primarily focuses on online meetings, many of the insights apply equally to in-person meetings.

When you have an online meeting with one or two team colleagues it's relatively easy to speak up and say what you want to say. But the bigger the group, the harder it is to make yourself known, especially when you are one of those people who like to sit quietly in a meeting and to ponder a bit more about subjects, rather than the 'shout it out loud' type.

Speaking up and getting noticed is not always easy for some individuals. People can feel uncomfortable during video calls for a variety of reasons. Being on camera can make people feel more self-aware and concerned about their appearance. They might worry about how they are perceived by others.

I know someone who experiences such strong self-consciousness about her appearance that she becomes almost paralyzed whenever she sees herself on camera or in photos. This discomfort is so profound that she frequently comes up with reasons to avoid being on camera altogether. She has even gone to the extent of claiming that the camera is malfunctioning or citing various technical problems. Seeing yourself on the screen can be distracting and even stressful for some people. To my surprise a lot of people still don't know you can hide the self-view in case that makes you feel uncomfortable. The camera sees you, but you don't see you.

Another problem with video calls is the lack of nonverbal cues that we can rely on in face-to-face conversations. This can make communication feel less natural and sometimes confusing; we are observing a lot of people at the same time and it can be exhausting. Without seeing the full context of social interactions, like where people are looking (lines of view), their body language and subtle facial expressions, it becomes more difficult to recognize natural cues about when it's appropriate to join in or interrupt a conversation. These visual signals help us gauge timing in social interactions, so missing them can make it harder to engage smoothly.

Making eye contact during a video call can be a challenge because it requires looking into the camera itself rather than directly at the faces of the people present. In a face-to-face meeting, you have the advantage of more direct eye contact and you can even use gestures to indicate the person you'd like to speak next, like subtly pointing at the chair to get noticed as the next speaker.

It's key to grab attention if you want to be heard, so here are some practical tips on how to do that.

Strategy 1: Know the reason why you want attention

The most important thing is to know why you want to grab the attention in a meeting. Everything starts with preparation beforehand. If you seek attention in a meeting without knowing why, you risk speaking just to be heard rather than to add value. You can be more intentional and impactful if you know why you want the attention. If you want to influence, be mindful of your style. If you want to challenge, come prepared with facts and figures. If you want to contribute, know what you want to add to the meeting.

Strategy 2: Start beforehand

You don't always have to solely bring up your topic during the meeting itself. Instead, you can take a proactive approach by sending an email to the chairperson beforehand, indicating that you'd like to address a specific issue. This allows the chairperson to allocate time for your topic on the agenda, ensuring it gets the attention it deserves.

Alternatively, you can email other participants to inform them about the subject you want to discuss. In your email, you can ask them to consider the topic in advance because you plan to share your opinion or present the key aspects of a project. And you can add that you would like to know their thoughts afterwards. This helps set a mindset for everyone that you will be the speaker on this topic. And it also allows for a more productive and informed discussion during the meeting.

Additionally, you can use the email to share your opinion on the topic ahead of time. This can help you clearly express your thoughts, which might be harder to do in an online meeting.

It's also worth considering technical elements ahead of time. You should make sure your equipment/professional image is in order. A crackly voice, a camera that shows a vague image, not being able to hear others because of broken earphones – we sure don't make a professional impression if we have the wrong equipment. Also make sure your computer is at the right angle.

I was once in a business meeting where a young person was slouched deep into the couch, almost melting into it like pudding, using her phone as her laptop. She lay back at an awkward angle, and the unsteady, shifting screen became a dizzying distraction for everyone watching. Since there was no medical reason for her position, it came across as unprofessional and sloppy.

Strategy 3: Choose your background wisely

If you want to be taken seriously, present yourself seriously. For instance, someone in a very serious meeting had this enormous mess behind him. Boxes stacked up, random knick-knacks everywhere, just total visual chaos. It was hard to focus on what they was saying because the background pulled all the attention. The messy background – cluttered and chaotic – undermined his credibility. It gave the impression that he was disorganized and possibly careless, which made it harder to trust his competence. Another time a person applied for a job with the interview being held online and they had a poster hanging on the wall in the background with an inappropriate slogan on it. It was supposed to be funny but in an interview the first impression was not good. Some people were definitely put off by the poster.

Your background creates an impression of who you are, what you do and what you consider important. We associate you with what we see, so make sure you show us the right things.

Strategy 4: Use your body language and move

Because we are so focused on movement it's very helpful to stimulate other people's visual cortex by movement and using body language to make yourself known.

Prepare your presence (posture, outfit, a clear desk and background). Other ways of grabbing attention online include raising your hand like we used to do in a classroom, sitting up straight so people know you are engaged, or even wiggling around a bit or nodding to grab attention.

You can also raise a finger, with your elbow on the table and your hand held out toward the camera, like signalling for a waiter, only a smaller, more subtle gesture than a full arm raise. Usually, a good chairperson or observant colleague will notice and respond to that gesture.

Strategy 5: Use your voice

Producing a sound is also helpful. You could clear your throat so people will pick up on the sound and realize that you would like to speak up. You could start by acknowledging the speaker before you by humming and saying yes to what he or she says. Or you could just ask if you are allowed to say something or, even better, just say something. For instance, 'I would like to elaborate on that' or 'I have a different view on that' or 'Could I ask how you see this happening in the field?'

As in any meeting, it's important to ensure you're heard by speaking at an appropriate and effective volume. Not everyone has a naturally loud voice, but when you speak, make sure it's audible.

Strategy 6: Stay focused

Make sure you stay as focused as possible. Of course, it can create a nice distraction if we see a glimpse of a cat or child during the meeting but in essence when you have a professional meeting, showing you are a professional is important. Yes, we might be working from home and can't always control our environment, like construction noise or crying children. It's important to consider the context of each meeting. Of course, a meeting with colleagues is different from one with a client, but staying focused is key. Avoid looking at your phone or staring out the window.

I always announce when I'm taking notes, so others understand why I'm not always looking at the camera. This helps manage expectations and clarifies my behaviour.

Some say to 'just be yourself', but you can be your professional self. If you want to be effective, make sure your behaviour reflects that.

Strategy 7: Dare to grab the attention

A good chair should give everyone equal opportunity to speak up. The chair needs to make sure all people are heard and not only the shouters. But if you have no chairperson or if you have a bad conductor of the meeting, you need to stand up for yourself. You need to stand out.

This last strategy has to do with the guts to do what you need to do. Grabbing attention online takes guts. It requires stepping out of your comfort zone and putting yourself out there in a way that can feel vulnerable. It takes courage to speak up, engage actively and use tools and techniques that might be unfamiliar at first. Understand that mistakes will happen and view them as opportunities to learn and improve. You have to get over the fear of judgment or criticism. In a virtual setting it's sometimes easier to stay muted and passive, but you need to have the guts to grab attention online.

You might even want to use emoticons to add a response to a story someone is telling, or post a comment in the chatroom, showcasing a touch of your personality in the digital conversation. It's about embracing challenges and using them as a spark to become more engaging, dynamic and effective in your virtual interactions. Each successful interaction will build your confidence and make it easier to take the stage next time.

Conclusion

While I strongly support live meetings, I understand that they are not always possible. When online meetings are necessary, make sure they are short, precise and professional. Make an effort, show yourself and contribute effectively.

PART THREE

Working with others

We are social creatures and even if you prefer working independently, it's almost impossible to find a job with no interaction whatsoever. Whether it's greeting the receptionist, participating in meetings or presenting to a group, we're constantly communicating with others. How we connect and work with people is essential to both our personal growth and professional success and every interaction is an opportunity to improve communication and build stronger relationships.

This part of the book is about improving your ability to work effectively with others, give and receive feedback and build stronger connections. It focuses on strengthening teamwork, actively listening and creating a positive environment. You'll come across situations that are unexpected – maybe a co-worker isn't responding or someone says something that belittles you. How you handle these moments can really impact the vibe of the workplace. Instead of waiting for others to change, it's about focusing on what you can do to encourage better cooperation. By being proactive and mindful in your approach, you can create a more supportive and productive atmosphere for everyone involved.

CHAPTER FIFTEEN

What to do if I want to give feedback to my colleague?

Many people find it difficult to give feedback to their colleagues. Providing feedback can be challenging for a variety of reasons, depending on your personality and the situation. I typically encounter three main reasons for this difficulty.

The first concern comes when people are afraid of a negative reaction from the recipient and therefore hesitate to share their feedback. They are uncertain about how their feedback will be received and if it will be seen as valid or relevant. They have a concern that the feedback might be dismissed or ignored.

The second concern is when people are afraid of upsetting others, causing conflict or facing consequences when they share their thoughts. This concern is even more real in situations where there's a clear hierarchy. It can be scary to give feedback when there's a big power difference. It might feel like speaking up could damage the relationship, be seen as disrespectful or even impact your position. In those moments, people often stay silent. This is an understandable human reaction.

Finally, in some cultures, giving feedback can come across as rude. Different cultures have their own norms, which can affect how open people are about sharing their thoughts and feedback with others. This all varies from business to business, but anyone is susceptible to these concerns.

Even those who truly want and are allowed to give feedback might not have the knowledge or skills to do this effectively. It requires clear and concise communication and some individuals may struggle with verbalizing their thoughts and concerns. It's one thing to know that someone needs feedback, but actually finding the right words can be tricky.

If you want to make feedback work, it helps to have an environment where people feel comfortable, respected and open to talk. In a workplace, that means having some ground rules for how feedback is given and received, making sure everyone knows how valuable constructive feedback is and maybe even offering tools or training to help people communicate better. Closer to home, you can improve your own skills by practising giving feedback and asking for it in return. Let's look at some strategies to achieve this. To me, feedback is about the development of behaviour and its impact. It's about improving collaboration, communication or performance not because something is wrong, but because it can be better.

When feedback gets a place in the organization, people know what they're doing right and where they can improve and work just gets smoother and more productive. If you provide feedback, communication becomes more effective and therefore the outcome of work will be more efficient.

Strategy 1: Observe

One of the main principles of feedback is focusing on actual behaviour. What do you see? What do you observe? What do you register? Think of it as something that could be captured on camera: clear, observable actions or behaviours. You should know that not all behaviour needs to be addressed when it comes to feedback. We have to observe effects the most. If the effect is as intended and wanted, you can reinforce the behaviour with positive comments and if you want a different outcome, you could give constructive feedback.

It's important to watch for patterns. One-off behaviours usually don't need feedback (unless it crosses a boundary – in which case, address it right away). A simple but effective approach is the following: if you notice a behaviour once, let it go – everyone has off days. If it happens a second time, make a mental note. But if you see it a third time, it's probably becoming a pattern and that's your cue to step in and give feedback. A precise and objective observation of the behaviour in question is key. When you observe and register observations, it allows you to gather concrete information and avoid misunderstandings that may arise from hasty judgments. Take notes of the specific actions, words or body language that you find concerning or problematic.

Strategy 2: Describe the behaviour observed or heard

When it comes to behaviour we want to change or improve, it's important to bring it up sooner rather than later. Timing and situation matter. Be mindful but avoid waiting too long. For instance, you wouldn't want to provide feedback to your colleague in front of a client. However, it's also not advisable to postpone until next month, when everyone's moved on from the situation. Make sure you are mindful of the context and setting and address the feedback as soon as possible in a setting that is safe and respectful for everyone involved. You might want to have a private conversation, stepping away from others in an office. Or if you can't leave the room, consider speaking in a hushed tone to avoid drawing attention.

So, what do you say? How to verbalize feedback in a way that is respectful, effective and so the person knows what to do and can apply the advised behaviour?

When you want to address behaviour, make sure you've observed the behaviour well. Being open and considerate in how you talk is important when you're handling behaviour-related problems. Avoid making assumptions based on hearsay or initial impressions. It's important to personally observe the behaviour or notice a recurring pattern when multiple people address someone else's behaviour.

When providing feedback, focus on the specific observed behaviour and its impact. Be both accurate and respectful. For example, if someone's behaviour is being labelled as 'unprofessional', identify the actions that led to that conclusion. Why would you use that label? In other words, what actions lead to that label? Is it related to not answering client calls, failing to submit project papers or consistently arriving late? It's crucial to pinpoint the exact behaviours we're observing. Sadly, many people throw out effects without being specific about the behaviour. Giving feedback is not a free pass to blurt out your opinion unfiltered. Furthermore, we need to be detailed in our observations. For example, when someone is late, we should clarify how late they are, as being one minute behind is different from being 30 minutes late. Clear, specific observations make feedback more effective and constructive.

Don't forget to give positive feedback to reinforce good behaviour, like saying, 'I noticed how you handled that client meeting – you were well prepared, with all the documents organized and the agenda clearly outlined, which made it easy for everyone to follow along and kept the discussion on track.'

For areas of improvement, be specific with constructive feedback, such as, 'Your ideas were excellent, but try slowing down when explaining complex points so that everyone has a chance to fully understand and keep up with the discussion.'

Strategy 3: Give clarity on the effect

To me, feedback is about the development of behaviour and its impact. It's about wanting to improve collaboration, communication or performance, not because something is 'wrong', but because it can be better. The question isn't, 'Do I dare to say this?' or 'Am I allowed to feel this way?' The question should be, 'Does this feedback contribute to improvement?'

Explaining the impact of someone's behaviour in your feedback is therefore important because it helps people to see how their actions affect you or others or even the company.

Describe the negative effects (or positive if you go for positive feedback) such as not meeting deadlines, the client's relationship of the project, the project's final outcome or the overall work atmosphere with colleagues.

Describing the effect their actions have makes the feedback more relatable and helps people to understand the issue better. You can also describe how their actions effect you personally – how they make you feel when they don't answer your email, for example:

> I've noticed that it often takes over a week to get a reply from you on emails – it has occurred five times now. It's starting to make me wonder about how much priority our collaboration is getting. It feels like our partnership might not be getting the attention it needs, and honestly, this has been pretty stressful for me.

Strategy 4: Connect it to the goal

Instead of simply pointing out behaviour you dislike, focus on the intended goal of the task, situation or interaction. Whether it's a presentation, collaboration, project or performance review you should suggest specific behaviours that could improve cooperation. Offering constructive advice on more effective behaviour is both pro-social and kind to everyone involved – it helps them improve, which ultimately benefits you too.

Describe the behaviour or outcomes you'd like to see. Be clear about what you'd like to change in how your colleague approaches tasks, such as handling the project, speaking with clients or cooperating with you:

> I really value our partnership and consistent communication is essential for us to succeed. Going forward, could you make it a priority to respond to emails within two days? Or, if it's easier, a quick call works too. This change is really needed to keep everything on track and make sure our collaboration stays effective.

Strategy 5: Be there to help

You can give a gentle reminder or nudge people to reinforce their new behaviour. For example, I know of a team leader who noticed one of their team members had trouble staying organized with daily tasks. Instead of letting them struggle through it, the leader spent five minutes each morning going over the day's top priorities with them. Some might call this handholding, but it was just enough support to boost their confidence. Within a few weeks, the team member started setting priorities on their own and the leader didn't need to step in anymore.

You can help change the behaviour and create positive change in the individual or the overall environment. It might take some effort but you will get results.

Strategy 6: Make sure the feedback is appropriate and ethical

Ethical feedback is all about being helpful, honest and respectful, with a real focus on the other person's growth. If it's sensitive, it's shared privately to avoid any embarrassment. In the end, ethical feedback is about giving input in a way that respects the person, encourages positive change and keeps their well-being in mind.

Feedback should focus on areas where a person can truly make changes, which often includes more than we realize. Even if it feels a bit uncomfortable or controversial, sharing thoughtful feedback can genuinely help others grow in ways they might not see themselves. So don't hold back – say it to help others but always be respectful and come from a place of goodwill. Make sure your intentions are clear and that your feedback is meaningful and actionable. Actionable feedback gives clear direction, so the person knows exactly what they can do to improve.

I was once hired to give feedback to an individual who seemed to neglect his personal hygiene. Initially, I hesitated to take on this task because of the sensitivity and personal nature of the topic. However, I decided to do it because it wasn't fair to the individual that no one in the company had the courage to address the issue. Everyone avoided the conversation out of fear, but providing this feedback was necessary for his well-being and professional development.

What was striking was that he sincerely valued my straightforwardness when we interacted. He had constantly wondered why people avoided getting close to him and why he felt like he was an outsider. That broke my heart. Because of the lack of courage of others, he hadn't been able to change the outcome of the interactions so far. Now that the problem had been acknowledged, he had at last been presented with the opportunity to change. He wholeheartedly embraced that chance and his contact with others (and therefore the work) improved.

Sadly, the fear of conflict is high in organizations. As a result, people often don't express their concerns, needs or irritations. I see this happening all the time: employees stay silent when something goes wrong. This silence can lead to situations worsening, gossiping and eventually things getting out of hand. Many people refrain from expressing their feelings due to fear of escalation, which only perpetuates the issue.

I believe it's kind to make the effort to help others grow. Remember, there's a difference between surface-level 'niceness' and true kindness. It's not 'nice' to tell a person that they have issues with their personal hygiene, but it is kind, as it's right for them to know about the issue so that they can address it. When I've explained this value in the UK, where giving feedback isn't very common, I've inspired quite a few people to give more feedback. One woman said, 'I never thought of it that way. I've just let them continue with their behaviour without ever helping them improve. That's actually not very kind of me.'

Strategy 7: Bring together all the points mentioned above

If you follow the guidelines above, you'll provide in-depth feedback with applicable advice. For instance, a poor example of feedback would be: 'Change your tone of voice when you talk to me!' This approach is disrespectful, very vague and is likely to provoke a difficult conversation.

Effective feedback should be specific, respectful and actionable. It should include what you have observed, the effect of the behaviour and the desired change for the future. For example, you might say: 'You are speaking very loudly right now and it feels intimidating when I try to have a conversation with you. Could you please use a softer tone? It would be very helpful, thank you.'

Be prepared to offer ongoing assistance to help increase awareness about the behaviour. Immediate change is unrealistic, so you may need to provide feedback multiple times. Additionally, giving friendly reminders can be very effective.

Imagine a colleague who often struggles with time management and misses deadlines. Explain the importance of meeting deadlines and using time wisely but also offer practical help. Share time management tips and tools or gently remind them when a deadline is approaching.

You could say: 'Feel free to ask for assistance if you'd like me to keep you informed in the future. I can provide friendly reminders. Just let me know if you'd like my help in keeping you on track.'

Conclusion

We give feedback to learn, to develop, to help ourselves and others and to contribute to a collaborative work environment. Having a thorough understanding of the behaviour will help you to approach the situation more effectively and empathetically. This approach allows you to focus on the relationship during the conversation because you have a clear understanding of the message you want to convey. The key is to address the issue as soon as possible, ensuring that the feedback stays relevant and timely. Be specific about what you want to communicate, so there's no ambiguity. Finally, offering support or assistance afterwards helps reinforce the relationship and shows that you care about their well-being. To summarize: speak up and move forward!

CHAPTER SIXTEEN

What to do if I want to become better at observing others?

'You see but you do not observe.' A famous quote from master observer and detective Sherlock Holmes, written by Arthur Conan Doyle. You might see things every day, but do you really notice them? There's a difference between just seeing something and actually observing it. When we observe, we not only notice our surroundings, but we also take in the details. When we observe, we also register. And when we register, we can use that information to make conscious decisions on how to act upon that information.

But how do you train yourself to focus on behaviour? Or what to do if you simply want to improve your ability to observe others as part of your job?

Strategy 1: Love people and their behaviour

It might sound obvious, but if you're not interested in others and would rather stay home with a book, it'll be harder to sharpen your observation skills. To get better, you need a real desire to observe and understand people, which means going out and applying what you've learned.

Many clients come to us with some foundation in human behaviour, whether from books, articles or videos online. There's a wealth of information out there – on group dynamics, leadership, meeting management or nonverbal communication. But keep in mind, while knowledge from books is useful, the real growth happens when you apply it in real-life situations. Watching people in action – in a restaurant, on the street or at work – gives you insights beyond what theory can offer.

Strategy 2: Peoplewatching

As an anthropologist you can study the behaviour of humans. Examining the cultures, languages and physical characteristics of people in various parts of the world. Like me, you can observe all of those topics while you are having something to eat or waiting for your plane at the airport. For a lot of people, a guilty pleasure is observing others when sitting at a restaurant or on a terrace, watching people pass by.

Looking at others will give you valuable information. The way people dress might give you information about their background, how they hold themselves may give you an indication of their self-awareness, how they use their hands or what they show with their facial expressions might show you their emotions. Their outfits might say something about their culture or their religion. Their posture might indicate something about their self-assurance. Their length of eye contact alone may provide hints about where someone is from, indicating their cultural background.

Maybe you even make up little stories about them. Are they father and son, colleagues, friends? Are they having a fight and have decided they are not talking anymore or are they just very comfortable around each other and feel no need to speak?

So much to see, so much to observe. It should be your joy to observe, to take notes and if possible to check your observation.

Strategy 3: Check your information

The tricky part about observing in real-life situations is that you can't always check things. Bias might not work in your favour. Only by asking will we be able to confirm our observation for sure.

So why not check? I've gotten into the habit of interacting with people whenever I can and it's led to some really great conversations. People love it when you ask questions in a kind and polite way and it helps you to check certain assumptions. 'You are tourists, aren't you? How do you like Amsterdam so far?' And with a question like that they tell you about their family visit and that this is the first time they are away together as father and son. Or other stories that have been shared with me. I observed a girl who seemed emotionally distressed after an intense conversation with a guy. Noticing her body language, I approached her to check if she was okay. She was very grateful and thanked me for checking in. She then started sharing her story, explaining that he had broken up with her. She said it was such a relief to be able to share it with someone. It's a special and honourable moment to get a glimpse of their life to maybe help them, and a brief moment for you to check your observation skills. Your passion for observing people should transform you into a proactive and focused observer.

Strategy 4: Watch TV

Another effective method to test and improve your observation skills, with a higher level of certainty to find out what's happening, is to watch a conversation from a TV show with the sound turned off. Make sure you watch it twice, first with the sound off. You observe the behaviour and try to make sense of what is happening. What are they talking about, what could be their relationship? Can we see a difference in status in how they approach each other? Do they act comfortable around each other? What is their emotion? Are they happy or sad? Sometimes a concentrating face can be mistaken for anger, or subtleness or sarcasm get lost without listening to the words.

The second time you watch the same material, you check your observations. Were they accurate? Preferably watch documentaries because reality shows often undergo significant editing and may not present events naturally or accurately. Documentaries typically aim to provide a more authentic and factual representation of the situation, offering a deeper and more genuine insight into real-life events and issues. Make sure you observe how individuals navigate and utilize the space around them; watch their proximity, their eye contact and their facial expressions.

Watching a talk show, for example, can be a great way to observe people discussing topics at the table. Nonverbal cues, like body language, add to our understanding, but they aren't the whole picture. We need to consider the context, content and the tone in which things are said. Don't rely solely on body language; listen closely to how something is said, noting the emphasis on certain words and the tone or volume of the text. Observation isn't just about seeing; it's also about hearing and understanding the layers in people's words and delivery. Look and listen to get the full picture!

Strategy 5: Role playing

Engaging in role-playing exercises, where you pretend to be someone else, opens up the opportunity to explore different facets of your own behaviour that may not typically surface.

This practice allows you to embody characteristics and responses distinct from your usual behaviour. Collaborating with a friend or colleague to practise various scenarios can provide valuable insights beyond the verbal content expressed – revealing nuanced behavioural patterns.

For instance, consider playing out a scenario where you take on the role of your boss as you are requesting a salary raise. By reversing the roles, you gain a unique perspective on how your boss might react and respond in such a situation. This exercise goes beyond verbal interactions; it helps you to become more attuned to subtle cues and behaviours that may be indicative of various communication styles and management approaches. In essence, these role-playing experiences become a powerful tool for enhancing your understanding of both verbal and nonverbal communication dynamics. As you explore different postures and gestures, you'll likely pick up on new body language cues, providing a fresh perspective.

Strategy 6: Talk to others

What are others observing? We all have our own background and experiences that we bring with us when observing others. We all observe details differently based on our knowledge and how we interpret things. The best part is talking about what behaviour catches your eye. What did you notice? What stands out to you? And is that the same thing as the person who is there with you, observing the same situation? When you ask them to share what catches their attention, what stands out for them, you'll get a better sense of how they view things, giving you new insights and information on observing others with a different perspective.

I love having conversations after seeing a play or movie to find out what stood out to the other person. We've watched the same performance, but it's always interesting to compare our observations – the differences, the similarities and the impact each of us felt. These discussions often reveal new perspectives for one another, making the experience even richer.

Strategy 7: Train yourself with puzzles

I love those puzzles where you have to find the seven differences between two pictures. They are a fun way to test my observational skills. Initially, you can start by taking your time to spot the differences, but as you get more into it, like me, you can set a time limit to challenge yourself to scan more quickly.

While *Where's Wally*, created by Martin Handford, is a classic way to train your scanning and observation skills, it can feel a bit old-fashioned today. A more modern approach might involve interactive games like the 'June's Journey' app, where you search for a variety of hidden objects, or the 'Find the Differences' game. It might not feel particularly business-like, but that's the point; these playful methods help you train essential skills in a way that's engaging and effective.

Conclusion

Real-world experiences teach you more than books alone ever could. So get out there, observe, take it all in and enjoy the lessons life offers. There are a ton of nonverbal cues to pick up on that help you understand the world around you. It's all about learning to connect what you know with what you see. The more you practise, the better you get at noticing subtle details you might have missed before.

CHAPTER SEVENTEEN

What to do if I want to connect with coworkers?

You might be working in a team but that doesn't automatically guarantee everyone's active participation. Not everyone possesses extroverted traits and is proactive when it comes to interaction. Some of you might prefer working from home or working secluded in a meeting room. However, engaging with others can bring you far.

Connecting with colleagues is not only enjoyable, it can also help you with productivity, goals and personal or team development. A lot of people find great joy in connecting with others once they find a way to do so. And even boring tasks can be more bearable when working with a supportive colleague or connected team. However, not everyone finds joy in this. Maybe you are a bit more of an introvert. And how can you reach out to that colleague always working from home or not present at the annual group outing? In this chapter we dive deeper into the strategies to connect more with others.

Strategy 1: Work on tasks together

An acronym of TEAM is Together Everybody Achieves More. And that is for a reason – it's a good reminder of the strength of collaboration. Working together on tasks enables individuals to benefit from diverse perspectives and insights. It creates a collaborative environment where team members can share ideas, brainstorm solutions and challenge each other's thinking. When you collaborate, you get to play off each other's strengths, making everything smoother and more fun. Plus, having those different viewpoints pushes you to think outside the box, bringing ideas you'd never come up with solo. Even if you are working on an individual task, sharing what you're working on or bouncing your ideas off a colleague can be great for teamwork. Keeping others in the loop about what you're working on helps everyone stay connected, and who knows – they might have insights or ideas to make things even better. They'll likely appreciate you reaching out, valuing their thoughts and inviting them to contribute.

Strategy 2: Start a conversation

Starting a conversation is a good idea because it helps you connect with others. You can share ideas and learn new things. But it's also an informal yet effective way to build relationships. You can help those people who are less likely to start a conversation themselves by asking them questions.

I once collaborated with a guy who struggled to initiate conversations. If you have trouble knowing how to start a conversation, try writing down a few go-to phrases to help you. We brainstormed various questions and conversation starters he could use, not only within his immediate team but also at company or network meetings.

Some examples included, 'What projects are you excited about right now?' or 'How did you get into your role here?' For more casual settings, he used starters like, 'What did you think about the drive here?' or 'Any good book or podcast recommendations?' These prompts gave him the confidence to start conversations more naturally.

In the beginning this sounded trivial, but it helped him to get over that hurdle to start a conversation. Closed-ended questions, eliciting a simple 'yes' or 'no', tended to halt the conversation. By asking open-ended questions, my client could delve into specific details and elaborate. Examples include: 'How did you spend your weekend?' 'Tell me about your family gathering last Thursday, how was it?' 'What were your thoughts on the project over the weekend?' or the old-time Dutch favourite, 'What do you think about the weather today?'

Strategy 3: Place food on your desk

This may seem like an unconventional piece of advice. However, it's surprisingly effective. When people gather around these shared items, it creates an opportunity for conversation, sharing of thoughts and exchanging of news. It's a small gesture that can have a great impact on building relationships and enhancing the overall atmosphere in the workplace. This can be a jar of candy on your desk, a crate of apples, a box of doughnuts or a bowl of fruit. Dutch scientist Louise Fresco said, 'Food, in the end, in our own tradition, is something holy. It's not about nutrients and calories. It's about sharing. It's about honesty. It's about identity.'

Strategy 4: Organize something

Many teams often complain that their annual team outing isn't enough. They want more. During training sessions, people often express their desire for more opportunities to connect and be together outside of work. But why rely solely on your employer for this? Why not take the initiative and organize it yourself? I've heard of people bringing in speakers to discuss specific topics, organizing after-work gatherings to tackle challenges and arranging events like bake-offs, fuddles, barbecues, picnics and even children's days with bouncy castles and face painters. Even online, teams have organized virtual cooking classes with one member leading as the chef while everyone else follows along, hosted pub quizzes or shared favourite songs through Spotify for a team playlist. The possibilities for creating fun experiences together are endless!

Yes, it costs time, it might even cost money. But the benefits are enormous. Meeting with your team in a different setting helps to create stronger connections.

Strategy 5: Ask for help and open up

Asking for help creates an opportunity to learn from others who may have more experience or expertise in a particular area, allowing for personal and professional growth. And it encourages teamwork and strengthens relationships within a group or community. If you ask for support, people are usually happy to give it to you. This support can be during a task in a project, but it can also be emotional support. Asking for help is a sign of strength, not weakness, and can lead to better outcomes both personally and professionally.

When you are tired, too busy or stressed it's helpful to share this with others. Let them know how you feel and what is going on in your life. It might not always be appropriate to tell them about your personal life but sometimes being vulnerable can be very effective in the workplace. It might help them understand you better and it creates more trust and deeper connections with those around you. It also allows others to support you when you're going through tough times or celebrate with you during happy moments.

It's also about leading by example. A manager I worked with noticed a shift in an employee's behaviour but assumed it was something personal and chose not to ask, as she herself preferred to keep personal matters private. After the employee resigned, she shared that her main reason for leaving was that her manager never checked in, even when she was clearly showing signs of struggling. This feedback opened the manager's eyes to the importance of creating space for employees to share or vent when needed, whether by asking, 'How are you doing?' or by occasionally opening up herself to show that personal things can affect us, too – it's not just all about work.

Strategy 6: Teach others

Sharing what you know with others is a great way to help them grow and to get engaged, both personally and professionally. Say you're good at data analysis and you spend some time showing a colleague who's just starting out. Not only are you helping them, but working together also opens up a chance to get to know each other better. You might find yourselves chatting more, not just about projects but also about everyday things – like their weekend plans, hobbies or family life. It's a win-win: you both learn something, build a stronger connection and have an easy point of contact going forward. What starts as a simple 'let me show you how' moment can turn into a great collaboration and even a friendship.

Strategy 7: Take an interest

People usually enjoy conversing and appreciate the attention. Connect with them if you know something important or exciting is going on in their lives. Ask how the new puppy is behaving or if the roof has been fixed. Or just simply ask how they are doing.

A manager struggled to keep up with everyone and wasn't naturally inclined to ask about people's lives. And because his team worked mainly remotely, he wasn't always able to observe how they were doing or have those little chats during lunch.

So together we created a system that worked for him. He simplified connecting by scheduling important moments. By noting down birthdays and important events, he ensured he didn't miss out on opportunities to connect. If for example he heard about an upcoming move, he noted the date in his agenda. This structured approach wasn't about being insincere; rather, it enabled him to genuinely connect with his team members during meaningful occasions. The effect was that during projects people were less hesitant to share problems or ask questions because they felt safe enough to approach the manager.

Conclusion

Whether you work remotely or see each other at the office every day, engaging with each other helps to create a better connection. When you take time to connect, you build trust and mutual understanding, which makes it easier to tackle challenges together. With that, your communication will improve, leading to more effective collaboration, a better work environment and very likely more fun! Plus, a connected team is more motivated and supportive, making work feel a little less like 'work' and a lot more rewarding.

CHAPTER EIGHTEEN

What to do if someone is belittling me?

If you've ever been belittled, you know how uncomfortable it feels. Even when you realize the comments are unfair, they can still make you feel small, inadequate and dismissed. Belittling shows up in various ways – through dismissive remarks, disregard for your thoughts or feelings or actions that subtly undermine your confidence and abilities. It's not just in the words used but also in the tone and nonverbal cues, like eye-rolling or smirking.

I once had a conversation with a professor and brought up two conflicting theories I had come across and wanted to hear his opinion about. His response initially made me crumble. 'But, sweetie,' he said (he actually said 'maar meisje' in Dutch, which translates to 'little girl' but with a connotation similar to 'sweetie' in how demeaning it felt). 'But sweetie (looking at me with a smirk), what do you know, you've only studied at the "University of Applied Sciences", not a "real" university.'

I recall feeling incredibly small and inadequate in that moment. However, I eventually figured out how to navigate the situation and I'm glad to share my approach here to help others, especially since many people (mostly women) have told me they've faced similar belittling behaviours. It's a story I've shared frequently and people have expressed to me how they wish they had responded as I did in that situation, recognizing it as a challenge they too often encounter.

First, I simply looked at him in a neutral way and asked, 'Sorry, what?' He repeated, 'Yeah... you've only been to the University of Applied Sciences.' That's when I decided to tackle his comment using two strategies: separating the content of what was said from how it was said. By carefully listening, I realized he'd stated a fact: I'd studied at the University of Applied Sciences. However, the way he threw in 'only' and called me 'sweetie' really did make my accomplishments feel smaller and left me feeling less valuable.

With that in mind I replied, 'Yes you are right. I've studied at the University of Applied Sciences. But why did you add "only" and "sweetie"? That comes across as if you want to belittle me and find what I do inferior.'

His eyes widened in surprise. 'Uh, no, I didn't mean it that way. I mean... well, no... what you do is entirely different, so you must possess different skills. I only meant that you might not be familiar with this theory in the way I am.' I then encouraged him to explain more, so we could engage in a meaningful discussion. This shifted his behaviour from dismissing me as a non-PhD to someone open to teaching.

I also work with trainees who are often faced with questions like, 'Can you make us coffee?' or are simply overlooked during meetings when questions are asked. They're frequently seen as people who are there only to learn, not to contribute.

So, what can you do if someone belittles you?

Strategy 1: Separate the message from its delivery

Start with listening. Take a moment to absorb both the content of what's being said and the manner in which it's delivered. It's helpful to separate the content of what is said from how it is said. By carefully listening and observing you can make a difference between the two. If you understand this difference, it allows you to address what matters.

Strategy 2: Verbalize

You might be in shock at first but don't let silence be your only response. It might help to give yourself some time to respond. A useful tactic is to momentarily pause and say, 'Sorry, could you repeat that?' This isn't just about getting a second to think it over but it also kind of puts the other person on the spot to think about what they just said. It gives you a moment to breathe, assess the situation and decide on the best course of action. This could mean you might want to address the comment directly, ask for clarification or steer the conversation in a different direction.

If you're caught off guard and don't know what to say, just say exactly that: 'I don't know what to say right now.' It's simple, but incredibly effective. I've seen this one sentence help people move through tension and continue the conversation. You can also verbalize your thoughts. I once left a business meeting to head to my next one. The man escorted me out of the office and began explaining how to navigate the streets, saying, 'Just look up and you'll see a sign on the wall that will let you know what street you are on.' I hadn't asked for his advice and of course I already knew how to read street signs. I couldn't help myself and, with a wry smile, said, 'I'm a grown woman; I do know how to read street signs, thank you.'

Strategy 3: Stand your ground

Standing your ground in these situations is essential because it reinforces your self-worth and resilience, allowing you to face challenges with confidence and composure. Internally, it keeps you connected to your value, while, externally, it shows others that you're strong and self-assured, helping you command respect. Differently said, you have to stand your ground emotionally and feel your worth. It's important to remember that others can only affect you as much as you permit. Personally, I draw strength from a line in the movie *Labyrinth*: 'You have no power over me.'

Externally, you also want to show your resilience. It's essential to demonstrate your strength. Maintain eye contact and show you are confident. Adopt a stance of presence and assertiveness. Even a small smile can reinforce your composure. Actress Robin Wright provides an excellent example of this kind of resilience. She shows it in the Netflix movie *Damsel* but also in the Netflix series *House of Cards*, where she plays the president. Wright perfectly embodies strength combined with a commanding smile. Her facial expression displays a flat affect, revealing little to no emotion apart from a commanding smile once in a while. Her neck is straight and her head held slightly high, with an open chest and shoulders pulled back. Her voice is slow in tempo, with a naturally low tone. I'm not here to discuss her character's tactics, I'm here to point out her nonverbal behaviour. She remains undiminished, showing the true nature of authority through her body language and presence.

Strategy 4: Focus on your achievements

Remind yourself of your core strengths and skills that have contributed to your successes. Don't let someone's negative comments overshadow your achievements and capabilities. Use their negativity as motivation to continue excelling. Reflect on the qualities that set you apart – whether it's your problem-solving ability, creativity or dedication, recognizing these strengths reinforces your value and helps you stay focused on your positive attributes. Instead of letting someone's negative comments overshadow your achievements, let it be a reminder of your determination to excel and continue striving for excellence. Sometimes they don't know you or your accomplishments, so their comments may come from a place of bias. This could actually be a great opportunity to share more about yourself and your achievements, helping them see your value and what you bring to the table.

Strategy 5: Ignore

When belittling happens, whether the person doing it is aware of it or not, ignoring the situation, the comment or even the person can be an effective response. You might want to avoid unnecessary tension or you don't want to give attention to something or someone that doesn't deserve it. When you ignore a remark completely, it sends a message that you're not letting it get to you – you're above it. It's like saying, 'I'm not letting this bother me.' This shows strength and control and puts you in a position where you don't feel the need to respond to every little thing.

A client I worked with was in a trainee position but was introduced as an intern. He decided to let it go in the moment since his manager was introducing him to the mayor. Correcting his manager would have felt awkward and the timing wasn't right.

However, this method of ignoring is often adopted out of a fear of confrontation. This sadly means disrespectful actions can continue because no one's calling it out when someone's putting others down. So, only choose to ignore as a deliberate strategy, not because you're hesitant to stand up for yourself.

Strategy 6: Use humour

I'm aware of a situation where a woman, being the only female in her team, was asked to prepare coffee for the guys for an upcoming meeting. She perceived this request as an attempt to diminish her role. However, her response was both clever and assertive. Rather than reacting with frustration, she decided to go above and beyond. She not only arranged for coffee but also purchased cakes, biscuits and even brought in a coffee machine for the meeting room. Furthermore, she crafted personalized coffee mugs for each team member. Setting everything up in the meeting room, she announced, 'Here you go, guys. Now we can all serve ourselves.' This move was a brilliant combination of compliance and empowerment, ensuring she made her point without a direct confrontation.

Strategy 7: Involve others

In a work environment, we face challenging behaviours, but this doesn't mean we have to face them alone. When you share your experiences with others, they can help you, they can provide support and potentially offer solutions. It can be a trusted colleague, a supervisor or a human resources professional. Speaking up about what you're going through can help address the issue more effectively and ensure you're not carrying the burden by yourself.

I worked with a team that was repeatedly belittled by another department, with their efforts often dismissed and their ideas overlooked and ignored in meetings. Tired of feeling undervalued, they decided to stand up for themselves as a group. They talked to their supervisor about what was going on and how it was affecting their work and morale. With the supervisor's support, they started sharing their successes more confidently in meetings and showing the value they added to the company. I helped them to present themselves and their ideas in a more effective way; their confidence and united front started getting noticed and others finally began to appreciate their hard work and skills. By standing up for themselves, they earned respect and improved their work environment.

Conclusion

Dealing with belittling comes down to how we handle it. Having confidence in ourselves and responding cleverly can really shift the situation. You don't have to put up with it, so don't be afraid to stand up for yourself and respond. A well-placed response can subtly remind the other person of your worth, without needing to escalate the situation.

Plus, if you handle it right, you might even help the belittler see the error of their ways and change their behaviour. Sometimes, calmly calling out the behaviour – like saying, 'I'd appreciate it if you'd take my input seriously' – can make them aware of the impact they're having. Even small actions, like maintaining eye contact and using assertive body language, can send a powerful message that you're not easily dismissed. Over time, responding with quiet confidence helps reinforce your value to others, making them think twice before undermining you again.

CHAPTER NINETEEN

What to do if your colleague or employee keeps making excuses?

If you are dealing with an employee or colleague who consistently underperforms and makes excuses, it can be extremely frustrating. When someone underperforms it not only slows down team progress and lowers the quality of work, it also forces others to take on extra tasks. This piles on extra work for the rest of the team, which often means more stress, some serious frustration and even potential burnout for those left picking up the load.

It can also create a sense of unfairness and sometimes it even leads to conflicts among team members due to the uneven distribution of effort and responsibility. For managers, handling underperformance adds extra work as well, taking up valuable time and energy that could be spent on other important tasks.

In one example, a team member who habitually arrived late would disrupt meetings with a loud and jovial 'Sorry, I'm late!'

Despite acknowledging themself being late, there was no change in behaviour. This led to irritation and frustration within the team, especially since no one, not even the team leader, addressed it directly with the person involved. Instead, people were gossiping about it, which only fuelled the frustration and tension among the team members.

If nobody addresses it, it can create distrust among team members. Especially if leaders don't deal with the problem, people might feel it's unfair and that there is no accountability for any behaviour. This doesn't just impact how the team works together in the short term; over time, it can lower team morale, slow down progress towards goals and damage trust between team members and leaders. If leaders don't step up, people don't feel safe.

When someone keeps making excuses, it's important to approach the situation constructively. Here are some steps you can take as a colleague, a team or a leader.

Strategy 1: Create clear goals in advance

We all have different preferences when it comes to leadership styles and it's important to consider culture as well. Are you more direct with your team or do you take a cooperative approach? And how do you approach your colleagues – do you encourage open dialogue or do you prefer a more structured, formal interaction? Whatever your company's style, one thing is key: make sure the goals you are working on are crystal clear and connected to the team's overall purpose.

If you are a leader, you can schedule a team meeting or, if needed, a one-on-one meeting in advance to discuss the team members' roles and responsibilities within the team.

If you notice behaviour that's full of excuses and lacks focus on goals, spell out what good, bad and totally unacceptable results look like. Once you both agree on these expectations, you can hold them accountable and give specific feedback if the work isn't meeting expectations. Clearly communicate what you require from your colleagues or the team, including deadlines, outcomes and standards. Make sure everybody understands the importance of their responsibilities.

Next, get on the same page about the process. Break down the steps needed to do their job well, maybe even walk them through it or ask what they need. And answer any questions they have early on to avoid future excuses about not knowing what to do.

Strategy 2: Find out why

It's important to delve deeper by asking open-ended questions to uncover the root cause if somebody is not working as expected or needed. 'Why are you always 20 minutes late?' or 'Why are you not meeting your goals?' can be helpful questions. Start by listening to their explanations without jumping to conclusions or immediate judgment. Sometimes, what initially appears as an excuse may actually come from valid concerns or obstacles that you hadn't previously recognized. Excuses often serve as a protective barrier. There might be underlying issues that individuals may be hesitant to tell you about directly. It's helpful to explore their reasons to gain insight. It helps determine if they're encountering challenges like a lack of confidence, skills, resources or motivation.

A manager brought up an employee's lateness and asked if everything was okay. After some hesitation, the employee explained they'd been caring for their ill partner each morning, which had caused the lateness. The manager responded supportively, suggesting options like a flexible start time to help balance work and personal responsibilities. The employee seemed visibly relieved and grateful for the understanding and flexibility, showing how open, supportive communication can make all the difference.

This approach not only creates a better understanding of the situation but also makes it easier to find constructive solutions that address the core issues at hand.

Strategy 3: Give feedback

We should communicate to people the impact their behaviour has on the work, yourself or others. This way, they'll understand how their actions slow everyone down and why it's important to do better. If they don't know, they can't change their behaviour. Give feedback that is specific, objective and focused on behaviour and outcomes, not personality (see Chapter 15).

Explain clearly what happens if they don't improve and what they gain if they do. That dialogue could look something like this:

> I've noticed that you've missed a deadline three times now. You often have an explanation, which I understand – things come up. But when it happens more than once, it comes across as avoiding ownership and it impacts the team's momentum. Meeting deadlines is a basic expectation, so I need you to take full responsibility and let me know early please if something might slip.

Strategy 4: Help them

If we know what the reasons are behind their excuses, we might be able to help them. Is the task too challenging for them? Are they bad at time management? Do they need training, other resources? Ask them what support they need to overcome their challenges and see if you are able and willing to offer it.

I know a manager who took the extra step of calling his employee every morning for a few weeks to ensure he arrived at work on time. When I share this story, many people react with scepticism, thinking it's excessive to call a grown man to wake him up. However, I always highlight the positive outcome it had. After just two weeks of this routine, not only did the employee establish a better routine for himself, but he also developed a warmer relationship with his manager. He expressed gratitude for the support and non-judgmental approach, which motivated him to take responsibility for his behaviour and improve his habits, such as using two alarm clocks placed in separate rooms.

As a colleague or manager, offering help might also involve leading by example: let your actions show how to tackle challenges. This shows others it can be done and might help them in the process. For instance, there was a colleague who struggled with filling out forms correctly during phone intakes, claiming there wasn't enough time to do it properly during the call. Another colleague decided to step in and demonstrate how she managed to fill out the form efficiently. By directly showing it was indeed possible, the initial reason no longer held up.

Strategy 5: Adjust their responsibilities

If things aren't working out, as a leader you may decide it's time to rethink an employee's tasks. Instead of letting excuses become a pattern, encourage a shift towards finding solutions. Each time they come up with an excuse, challenge them to propose at least one solution to their problem. If necessary, consider reassigning some of their tasks to better align with their capabilities. This might be temporarily to reduce them being overwhelmed.

Someone who had previously performed well in supporting project roles and client communication was given the opportunity to lead a project. But the transition proved more challenging than expected. While they had strong content knowledge and good communication skills, they struggled with key project management tasks such as setting clear priorities, keeping stakeholders aligned and guiding the team through uncertainty. Over time, both the client and internal team voiced concerns.

To keep the project on track, the responsibilities were adjusted. A more experienced project manager took over the leadership tasks like overseeing timelines and coordinating the team's workflow, while the original project lead remained responsible for client communication. This allowed the project to move forward smoothly, while still recognizing the person's strengths and contributions.

Strategy 6: Create awareness and self-reflection

The feedback may not only focus on their content or goals but also on their overall approach to life. It's important to address how their actions affect both others and their own professional development. Encourage them to reflect on why they often resort to making excuses.

I once coached a girl who was seemingly lacking in work ethic. She kept saying, I can't do this, I'm not able to do this. But through self-reflection she realized that her excuses stemmed from a fear of failure. When I confronted her about how not taking action was actually a form of failure, it served as a wake-up call for her. This motivated her to work on her self-esteem. She changed her behaviour by taking on her responsibilities and confronting her fears head-on. This change in her behaviour not only drove her towards her goals but also enhanced her self-confidence and her ability to manage setbacks effectively.

Strategy 7: Know when to draw the line

Sometimes enough is enough. You have to let people know in advance what's at stake. Explain how doing their job successfully can create opportunities and build their reputation. On the flip side, not getting the job done will have consequences. If, after support and opportunities to improve, the behaviour doesn't change, it may be necessary to take more formal steps depending on the context. Then maybe you need to have that difficult conversation and part ways. Sometimes reaching a breaking point is unavoidable.

Conclusion

With these actions, you can help your colleagues or employees to step up their game and create a more productive work environment. Remember, the goal is to create a safe culture of accountability and growth that benefits everyone involved. Keep motivating and supporting your team towards excellence but don't be afraid to set boundaries along the way!

CHAPTER TWENTY

What to do if someone doesn't respond?

One of the things I find challenging is when someone doesn't respond after I've asked a question. Whether it's during a meeting, a conversation or even in written communication like emails, I've noticed that waiting for a reply can sometimes feel like a long time. In face-to-face interactions, this can be especially tricky because you're left in a moment of silence, wondering if the other person needs more time to think or if they simply didn't hear or understand you. People process information at different speeds and what seems like a long pause to one person might just be the other person gathering their thoughts.

However, there are still times when you don't get a response at all. It's as if a question just doesn't stick, like it's slipping through the cracks. When that happens, it creates an awkward silence that's hard to ignore. You're left wondering if you should repeat yourself or just move on and that uncertainty can feel uncomfortable.

The same goes for emails. You ask a question or take the time to respond to someone's question, but then you don't hear anything back. It can be a bit frustrating, especially when it happens with companies whose services I'm genuinely interested in using. We all understand that everyone's busy and that responses might not always be immediate. However, it's still surprising – and a little disappointing – when there's no reply at all. It leaves you wondering if your message was lost or simply overlooked. In a world where communication is so crucial, a simple acknowledgement can make a big difference.

Here are some strategies that might help when you don't get a response.

Strategy 1: Check for errors

I remember a story about a manager who got really upset with a colleague for not replying to his email, only to realize later that he had never sent it to her in the first place. It's a good reminder to always double-check your contact details – make sure the email address is correct before assuming someone didn't respond. For example, mistyping an email address, like using .com instead of .eu, or missing just one letter in the name, can easily prevent your message from being delivered. And did you check your spam folder? You might have already received a reply, but it's hidden in your inbox. The same goes for phone calls or text messages, of course.

Strategy 2: Be patient

A good friend of mine is a wonderful person, but also quite impatient. He once sent an email to a company and expected a reply the same day. While quick responses are great customer service, that's not always how things work. Unfortunately, companies don't always communicate when a reply can be expected, which can lead to frustration. Simply letting the customer know the expected response time can make a big difference in their patience. An out-of-office reply is particularly useful in these cases, as it provides a clear idea of when to expect a response.

It's important to give people a fair amount of time to respond to an email, since response times can vary depending on the company and culture. For instance, I like working with Americans because they usually reply quickly, often within a few hours. But it's good to keep in mind that everyone's busy and might have other priorities, so it's usually best to wait a bit before following up.

When it comes to patience it's just as important in conversations. When someone doesn't respond immediately, it's crucial to give them time to process what you've asked. They might stay silent for a while or answer in a way that you think is not focused on the question at all. I once asked a coachee a question and before answering, she spent 10 minutes talking about something else. I realized she needed to get that off her chest before addressing my original question.

Also, a dear friend almost replies to a question with a storytelling. If I ask him, 'Would you like some coffee?' his reply is usually indirect: 'I went to my aunt's house for her birthday yesterday. It was such a nice gathering! Everyone was there and we had the most delicious cakes. My aunt really outdid herself this year. We all sat around the table, chatting and laughing.'

It used to take me a moment to figure out how on earth his story would answer my question and, at first, it left me confused – where is this going? But I've learned that if I just wait, he'll eventually get to his point. I'm used to it now and I know to give him the time he needs to respond. He would end with: 'We had such a good time, and, honestly, I think I had more coffee than I usually do in a week. So, to answer your question, no coffee for me right now, thanks. I think I'll go for some tea instead.'

My impatience definitely has a cultural side to it. In the Netherlands, when you ask a question, you usually expect a quick, straightforward answer. That's just how we're used to communicating – clear and to the point. When I started working with people from different cultures, I quickly realized that's not always how things work. In some cultures, answers can come wrapped in stories or take a bit longer to get to the point. I had to adjust my expectations and learn to go with the flow, appreciating that people communicate differently depending on where they're from. It's helpful to be more patient and open-minded in conversations. Patience truly is a virtue.

Strategy 3: Follow up

Whether it's in an email or during a conversation, if someone doesn't respond, it might be because they didn't fully understand your request, or it got lost in the flow of the discussion. In the case of an email, they may have overlooked it because of their busy schedule.

For example, if you've asked a colleague for feedback and haven't heard back, it's possible they missed your request or are swamped with other tasks. A polite follow-up message can make all the difference. A gentle reminder helps bring your request back to their attention without seeming pushy.

You could write something along the lines of this:

> I hope you're doing well. I just wanted to follow up on my previous email regarding [specific request or project]. I know you're busy, so I completely understand if it slipped through the cracks. Whenever you have a moment, I'd really appreciate your feedback/input.

Strategy 4: Be clear and direct

If it's important, don't hesitate to be more direct in your follow-up. You can express the urgency while staying polite. When I suggest this method, some are reluctant, fearing it might cause escalation. Being direct might be a Dutch approach, but I've seen too many projects go off track because people were hesitant to push a little. However, the reality is that problems can also escalate if you don't address them head-on.

A more direct email could be:

> I hope you're doing well. I'm following up on my earlier email about [specific request or project]. I understand you're busy, but I need your feedback/input as soon as possible to keep things moving. Could you please share your thoughts by [specific deadline, e.g. end of day tomorrow]? If there's anything causing a delay, let me know, and we can work through it. I appreciate your prompt attention to this!

Strategy 5: Use a different method

If your initial contact was through email and you haven't received a response, you can consider reaching out through an alternative method. A phone call, text message or even a LinkedIn message can sometimes be more effective. People may overlook or miss an email, especially if they're busy, but a direct call or message on another platform can grab their attention more effectively. Additionally, using a different method for how you reach out shows you're flexible and serious about connecting, which can be helpful when things are time-sensitive or urgent.

If someone isn't responding during a conversation, try rephrasing your question or comment to make it clearer. You can also help them by asking if they need more time to think about it or if there's something they'd like to discuss first. Sometimes, changing the conversation slightly or asking a related question can help them feel more comfortable and engaged, encouraging a response. Additionally, using nonverbal cues like maintaining eye contact, leaning in a bit or nodding can signal that you're patiently waiting for their input.

Strategy 6: Involve a third party

If you're not getting a response and it's affecting your work progress, you might need to involve someone else to move things forward. For instance, if an email goes unanswered and it's holding up a project, you could reach out to a mutual contact or a supervisor who can help facilitate communication and ensure the issue is addressed.

In a meeting, if one person isn't responding to a question or concern, you could try asking someone else's opinion to keep the discussion going. This keeps the conversation on track and encourages participation. The original person might engage as well after that. If you involve others, you can often find a way to get things done or get the answers or actions you need without letting things stall.

Strategy 7: Move on

If they still don't respond after multiple attempts, it might be time to move on or try a different approach. I've been in situations where, despite my efforts, I received no reply. I believe it's important to let someone know if something went wrong or why you don't (are not willing to) respond. Usually, clear communication keeps things moving and gives people the closure they need, instead of leaving things hanging. Even a simple 'no thank you' or saying you're too busy would help everyone move on more easily. We need contact, not ghosting.

However, while it's easy to take it personally and feel frustrated, it's important to remember that there could be various reasons for the lack of response. If someone isn't engaging, it's probably a sign to let it go and focus your energy elsewhere. This goes both for emails and for conversations – if it's not working, sometimes it's best to just stop and move on.

Conclusion

We're all human, and with how busy things get, it's easy to forget stuff.

Sometimes people don't respond because they're busy, overwhelmed, unsure how to reply or simply didn't like the question. For example, if they receive random sales emails or inappropriate questions, they may not feel the need to respond. When someone isn't responding, first follow up politely and give them some time. If there's still no reply, consider reaching out through a different method or asking if there's a reason for the delay. Ultimately, it's up to you to decide how urgent the matter is and how you want to handle it.

CHAPTER TWENTY-ONE

What to do if I want to become a better listener?

We all know how wonderful it feels to tell a story while people really focus on us, giving us their undivided attention. In those moments, you truly feel heard, seen and validated. It can be frustrating when someone goes into solving mode straight away or looks at their watch with an impatient look. This lack of attention can make you feel dismissed and unimportant.

In the busy moments of life, we might not always give that level of attention that is needed in these situations. Listening with care is easier said than done, but it's essential for meaningful communication. Taking the time to truly listen can make a huge difference. It shows respect for the other person and makes them feel valued.

Good listening isn't just about hearing words; it's about being present, showing empathy and making the speaker feel important. By actively listening, you acknowledge the speaker's feelings and experiences. And of course, listening well can prevent misunderstandings and conflicts. If you can put this skill into action, you can build trust and strengthen relationships, both personally and professionally.

So here are some things you can do to help you enhance your listening skills

Strategy 1: Pay full attention

Put away distractions like your phone or laptop, remove your earplugs and give your full attention to the person speaking. Though we all know this, it's surprisingly rare for people to actually take off their headphones or put their devices aside. One woman shared how her boss often walked into conversations still wearing large headphones. She said, 'Even if they're off – which I can't tell – it distracts me and makes me feel like he's not really paying attention.'

Some restaurants have introduced 'Mobile Free Meals', offering customers a discount off their food bills if they give up their phones. Phones will be locked in cash boxes on the tables, with staff holding the keys – the idea is to enhance interaction and minimize distractions. All too often you see people with devices in their ears. Make sure you're in a setting that helps you focus on listening. Minimize background noise and other distractions that can interfere with your ability to listen effectively.

Strategy 2: Show that you're listening

There are conversations you might remember where people started staring out the window, gazing behind you or into a void or fixating on their notes, computer or phone. They might have been listening, but it sure didn't feel like it.

In the 1970s, Edward Tronick conducted the 'Still Face Experiment', where a mother was instructed to stare at her baby with no expression for several minutes. The effect was a crying, desperate baby (Streep, 2023). Recently, a similar experiment was conducted involving smartphones, with the background idea of parents looking at their phones in front of their baby, resulting in less facial expression. The babies also responded negatively to this behaviour. This raises the question: what happens when we, as adults, look at each other with no expression?

While the effect on adults might not have been extensively studied at universities, empirical observations and probably your own observations suggest that it is indeed frustrating when someone looks at you with no expression, whether they are looking at their phone, staring out the window or looking at notes on the table. To create better interactions, make sure you maintain eye contact, show a head tilt during conversations, smile when appropriate; even nodding can encourage the other person to talk more. I would say, 'Set down the device and make your attention precise.' To be a good listener, make sure you're genuinely engaged. Maintain eye contact, nod occasionally and summarize what is being said. This not only shows that you are listening but also makes the speaker feel valued and heard.

Strategy 3: Avoid interrupting

This is something that can be challenging. When you're enthusiastic, especially when someone tells a great story you can relate to, you naturally might want to know more and start asking questions. Similarly, when someone is showing their emotions, you might feel the need to ask a lot of questions to understand them better and help. However, balancing your enthusiasm or helpfulness with attentive listening can make a big difference in how the other person feels. Let them finish their thoughts without interrupting, as interrupting can be frustrating and disrupt their flow of ideas. I've taught both others and myself that sometimes you just have to zip it and listen.

Strategy 4: Use your words wisely

By summarizing what the speaker has said, you can ensure that you've understood correctly. Pay close attention to the order and emphasis of the information that is shared. What they mention first or repeatedly can indicate what is most important or urgent to them.

Use their language and phrases like 'So what you're saying is...' or 'It sounds like you're feeling...' to reflect back on what you've heard. If you use the words the speaker uses, it will build rapport and trust. It not only shows that you are actively listening but also helps to clarify any misunderstandings.

For example, if a colleague says, 'I just feel like nobody respects my input in meetings', you could respond with, 'I'm sorry you feel like nobody respects your input in meetings.' You could also say, 'I'm sorry to hear that you feel that way. It must be frustrating to feel like your opinion isn't being valued.'

When you paraphrase, you show the speaker that you are engaged and paying attention to their words. It also provides an opportunity for the speaker to correct any inaccuracies in your understanding, leading to clearer and more effective communication.

It shows respect for their perspective and acknowledges their experience. It confirms that their message is being received as intended. This is particularly important in sensitive or emotionally charged conversations, where feeling understood can significantly impact the speaker's comfort level and willingness to share openly.

A manager once tried to paraphrase someone by saying, 'I hear you're sad'. The person responded, 'Sad?!? I'm livid!' He had completely missed her body language and clear words like 'frustrated' and 'angry'.

Strategy 5: Dive deeper into the talk

You can show your interest by asking questions. This not only clarifies your understanding but also shows that you are engaged and interested in the perspective of the other person. When you ask questions, it encourages the speaker to elaborate on their points. This can lead to a deeper and more meaningful conversation. It helps you to gather more information, gain better insights and can lead to a deeper conversation. Try to ask open questions like 'Why', 'How', 'What', 'When', 'Where' and 'Who'. These types of questions encourage detailed responses and foster deeper engagement. Open questions can also help uncover underlying thoughts and feelings, providing a richer understanding of the speaker's perspective.

I've heard a story about someone who got fired and initially responded in a detached manner, focusing on the procedure while sharing the information with colleagues. It wasn't until someone asked, 'But how does all of this make you feel?' that they were able to open up and let their emotions in. This simple, empathetic question helped them connect with their feelings and share their true experience.

Strategy 6: Empathize

You might not always agree with what someone is saying but you can empathize with them on how they feel or how things must be for them.

Try to understand the speaker's feelings and perspectives by putting yourself in their shoes and responding supportively. Use statements like, 'I can understand why you feel that way' to show empathy. You might say, 'I can see you're upset. It must be tough to hear that feedback. Do you want to talk about it? I'm here to listen.'

After they share their feelings and you listen with care, you can say, 'I understand why you feel this way. It's hard to receive criticism, especially when you've worked so hard. Your dedication is clear, and I believe we can use this feedback to improve and highlight your strengths. Let's figure out a plan together to move forward.'

Strategy 7: Slow your pace

Good listening requires patience. You must give the other person the time to express their thoughts fully before responding. Avoid rushing them or finishing their sentences for them. For instance, a manager once hurried through a brainstorming session, not giving team members the chance to fully explain their ideas. Later, it turned out that many team members had good ideas to solve the problem at hand, but these ideas were only gathered after the manager had left. This highlights the importance of slowing down and giving everyone the opportunity to share their thoughts.

Conclusion

Listening will help you to create a connection with others but it's also effective for a more efficient and productive work setting. Becoming a better listener is important for effective communication and it helps to build relationships. People notice when someone actually takes the time to tune in. It even creates a more comfortable, productive vibe at work because people feel valued and understood.

And becoming a better listener can sometimes reveal things you never expected, like a hidden idea or a solution to a problem you hadn't seen. So, when you take the time to really listen, everything flows better, people open up more and work gets smoother. It may take a bit of practice, but it's worth the effort.

PART FOUR

Leadership

I've spoken to many people who share their frustrations about poor leadership: leaders who don't make an effort, who don't validate, who are unaware of their influence. We need to do better.

I once had a realization while sitting in a coffee shop: good leadership is a lot like being a barista. First, you have to recognize that everyone likes their coffee differently. When I travel, I have a little ritual at Schiphol Airport where I order a Grande decaf latte with an extra shot of decaf at Starbucks. Then, I sit down and observe other travellers. Almost everyone orders a different coffee: a latte with cream, an Americano, a caramel latte with whipped cream, a flat white, a cappuccino or a macchiato. There are so many options: different types of milk, sugar or no sugar and some might even opt for tea, matcha or a soda. And even when people order the same drink, they consume it differently. I once saw a guy stirring his whipped *cream into the cup until it dissolved before he drank it. Another person ate the whipped cream off the top before drinking, while someone else drank it right away, leaving a whipped cream mark on their nose.*

As a leader, you must recognize that everyone has different preferences and it's your job to pick up on those. Some people may need a direct approach to leadership, while others might prefer to be more independent, knowing they can come to you with questions if necessary. In this analogy, the coffee represents the idea that everyone has different needs, even in their daily routines. Think of it like that coffee: while everyone might drink it, they each enjoy it differently. Similarly, every team member may need leadership, but in a style that suits their individual preferences.

CHAPTER TWENTY-TWO

What to do if you are starting a new job as a leader?

When beginning a new job, many people are filled with enthusiasm. However, in their eagerness, they often neglect to take the necessary steps to ensure a strong start. As a leader, starting off on the 'right' foot is key and that means figuring out some crucial details before diving in. Onboarding can look really different depending on where you are. Some companies have detailed programmes, while others just throw you into the deep end. No matter how much formal or informal onboarding you get, it's important to keep a few strategies in mind. They might sound simple, but you'd be amazed at how many people skip these basics when starting a new role.

Strategy 1: Inform yourself about the rules

Make sure you have a clear understanding of policy guidelines. Too often people don't know what is allowed or not. Knowing the rules helps you to ensure that you and your team operate within the boundaries set by the company. It also helps you to make better decisions that align with company policies and objectives. If you show you understand and follow the rules you will earn the trust and respect of team members, colleagues and stakeholders. It enhances your credibility and fosters a culture of accountability, fairness and respect within the organization. A great question to ask is: 'What is the number one rule people forget about in this company?' Or phrased differently: 'What is the number one mistake people tend to make in this company?' Ask every division, especially HR and compliance.

If it's a smaller company, take the time to ask individuals separately; you'd be surprised by the range of answers you get. It's a simple way to uncover potential pitfalls and understand what really matters here, even if it's not written in the handbook. You could ask questions like: 'What's one thing you wish you'd known when you started here?' or 'Are there any "unwritten rules" around here that people don't often talk about?'

Strategy 2: Inform yourself about the past

Informing yourself about past events, challenges and successes within a company is essential. It will give you a valuable context that helps you understand the company's culture, values and views on certain things. It will also give you insight into how people approach the past. Are they willing to share about the past, are they negative, hesitant, do they hold grudges or are they full of energy, proud of what has happened and who they work for?

Don't just ask about product history or key decisions, but also about significant events involving employees. It's important to be aware of major changes with staff, conflicts and even notable gossip. The last one might feel inappropriate, but we have to understand that gossiping will happen. It's up to you as a manager how you deal with it but by noticing what is talked about in the office you might get some information that needs to be investigated. Understanding and listening to people who describe the company's history helps you identify patterns and make informed decisions to avoid repeating past errors. Being aware of past events fosters transparency and trust among colleagues and stakeholders, because it demonstrates your commitment to understanding the organization's journey.

A new team leader I worked with asked her colleagues about her predecessor and discovered that this person had been a real bully, something HR hadn't mentioned during her job interview. This was crucial information because the team was damaged, scared and hesitant to show initiative due to past experiences. The new leader needed to ensure the team felt safe moving forward.

Knowing both the company's history and its social dynamics helps you contribute better to its future and build stronger connections with colleagues.

Strategy 3: Inform yourself about the company culture

What are the dos and don'ts within this company? While values might be written down somewhere, ask people about the three main values they think are important within the company to understand what they truly embody. Asking questions like 'What is the best thing someone has ever done?' or 'What is the worst thing anyone has ever done?' can provide insights into the company culture and what people consider outstanding or important. What are the values according to them?

At a large company I worked with, their values 'Respect, Kindness and Honesty' were prominently displayed on posters throughout the office. However, when I asked employees about these values, many responded with smirks and made it clear that 'respect and honesty' was not practised at all. They shared that management often withheld information. When employees asked questions or sought clarity, responses were often vague or delayed, leaving them feeling left out and with the sense that there was a lack of honesty. They also mentioned that being treated with respect wasn't truly present in their day-to-day work environment. Team members were routinely cut off or ignored when offering input. It was a crucial issue that required attention during the behavioural change project.

Strategy 4: Make a difference between paper versus practice

People might read the guidelines of a company, but paper is different than practice. The posters on the wall might say there is an open feedback culture, but you will only know for sure if you've observed that behaviour actually happening in real life. Rarely do starting leaders observe others for at least a full day (longer if possible) without intervening or commenting. I advise them to simply observe a day in the life of the company without interacting.

When one new leader did this, it was initially awkward for others, but they eventually forgot about him during the meeting. By the end, the leader was pleased to have noticed some patterns that might need some extra focus in the future. Through observation alone, he gained valuable information.

Strategy 5: Inform yourself about the expectations

Understanding the expectations others hold for you in a new job is crucial for your performance and integration. When you have clarity on your roles and responsibilities, you will gain smoother collaboration and communication, not just from the people who hired you like your supervisors but also from your colleagues and the people on your team. If you dare to ask about the wants and needs of your team or individuals it builds trust. The team members might have been used to a certain style of leadership and it is great to find out if those expectations match yours. By knowing if you can and are willing to meet or even exceed these expectations, you can not only avoid conflicts, you can also pave the way for growth and development within your team. By knowing what they want and need you can align your behaviour. Ultimately, being aware of and responsive to others' expectations sets the stage for successful navigation of the workplace environment and achievement of your career goals. I believe powerful questions to ask are, 'How do you prefer to be led by me?' and 'What should I avoid when leading you?' That doesn't mean you have to do everything they ask, but you can treat it as useful input.

Strategy 6: Building up relationships

Yes, you are starting a new job and yes you might be eager to dive into the content of it all. But make sure you first work on your network within the company. Have lots of coffee moments, have lunch with many different people and avoid the temptation to settle into one particular group too quickly. Be proactive in scheduling 'getting to know you' conversations with as many colleagues as possible.

When talking to new people, be sure to ask them who they think you should speak to next. This question helps you discover the company's internal network. Who communicates with whom, who's frequently mentioned and even who might be left out. All of this takes a lot of time and that's usually why it's not done very often. But those who do take the time and opportunity create a wonderful foundation of knowledge, interaction and contacts.

Strategy 7: Properly introduce yourself

I heard about someone who started giving feedback on the job before anyone even knew who he was. Their first encounter wasn't pleasant. Without an introduction, people received negative feedback and comments on their work from this new person, not even knowing who he was. Each company introduces new people in its own way, but it's always helpful to make sure others know who you are. Whether you're introduced through a newsletter, an email or at a team lunch, plan ahead so you can make a memorable first impression.

Share a bit about yourself: start with your name, where you're from and your role, then give a glimpse into your approach to the job and what excites you about it. I would also advise to add a personal touch, although that is not appropriate in some settings. If you want, you could mention something about your family, pets, hobbies or an interesting part of your background. These small details can go a long way in helping others feel connected to you right from the start.

Don't forget to take your crowd into consideration. I heard a story about a new manager who started her first presentation with a breathing yoga exercise in a room full of factory workers. Her intention was likely to create a relaxed, welcoming atmosphere, but the approach missed the mark. Many of the workers weren't familiar with or interested in yoga and they felt uncomfortable, frustrated and even angry with being asked to participate in an exercise that didn't resonate with them. They later described it as out of place and irrelevant to their daily work. This disconnect between the manager's approach and the audience's expectations created a sense of awkwardness. Instead of breaking the ice, the exercise just highlighted how out of touch she seemed, setting an uncomfortable tone for the rest of the session – a rough first impression that made it hard to build trust right from the start.

Conclusion

Starting a job can be fun and complicated at the same time. There's a lot to be learned and a lot to find out. Make sure you not only follow the official onboarding programme but that you are a proactive, professional and warm investigator who is eager to learn about the new company with its background, values, people and goals. By finding out more in the beginning of your job, you can align your working goals with what is needed and wanted. A good start is half the battle.

CHAPTER TWENTY-THREE

What to do if I need to conduct a meeting?

At work you have meetings almost every day. This could be online, hybrid or in a live face-to-face setting. The purpose of most meetings is to come together, cover important topics, share updates, make decisions and then move forward with any tasks that come from that session. It's an important setting for collaboration and a way to ensure everyone is on the same page. But it also allows you to create new ideas and solutions or to see how people are doing.

In my years of assisting companies in becoming more effective, I've observed that many issues with ineffective communication often arise during meetings. These issues can include people failing to attend, not being focused during the meeting or not actively contributing and remaining silent (as discussed in Chapter 14).

Ineffective meetings are often the result of poor meeting management. The person designated as the chairperson is typically not trained in how to lead a meeting effectively. This can easily lead to frustrating experiences where discussions drag on, people repeat themselves, time runs out and decisions are endlessly postponed. We've all had those long-lasting meetings with people repeating themselves, deviations from the agenda or reccurring subjects. When I bring up ineffective, drawn-out meetings in my teaching sessions, it always gets a laugh of recognition. Or as a participant once said: 'Meetings at my company? Pure torture! They go on forever, nothing gets decided and it makes me question all my life choices!'

While everyone is responsible for creating an effective meeting, as the chairperson, it's your job to keep things running efficiently. Here are some strategies to help.

Strategy 1: Prepare

Although this may sound trivial, it's surprising how many individuals fail to prepare adequately for meetings. As the chairperson, it's even more crucial to have a clear understanding of what you want to achieve and how you plan to steer the meeting. You bear the responsibility for managing time, location and the ultimate outcome of the meeting. While you can't control the level of content contributed by others, an effective chairperson is proactive, maintains structure and drives the discussion towards a solution when needed.

Depending on the meeting, it's important to plan ahead. In advance, identify topics that require more time or may be sensitive and plan your meeting accordingly. If a topic is sensitive, take the time to prepare how you'll set a respectful and professional tone. For instance, you can begin the meeting by stressing the importance of open communication, active listening and mutual respect among all participants. As an example, you can say: 'As we tackle this sensitive issue, let's focus on open communication, active listening and mutual respect. Please, no interruptions or negative comments, to keep our discussion productive and respectful.'

Strategy 2: Observe the room

Whether it's online or in person, nonverbal communication plays a crucial role in understanding interactions. As facilitators, it's essential to observe body language and other nonverbal cues that participants display. These cues help you understand underlying emotions and concerns that are not expressed verbally. Do we see two people whispering while someone is talking, is someone on their phone during an explanation of a topic? In online meetings, these observations are just as important as they are in person. Are people slouching? Is there eye rolling, nostril flaring? These are all cues we should observe to gain insight into the dynamics of the interaction. As a chair, it's important not only to notice this behaviour but also to act. For example, if everyone seems tired, you could consider creating a short coffee break.

Strategy 3: Create turn-yielding

There are many examples of meetings where someone has a very long monologue and everyone just sits there. Nobody steps in or tries to redirect, so by the end, frustration is at an all-time high. Every now and then, someone realizes they could've nudged the chair to step in. But more often, the gossip kicks off about the cluelessness of the person doing the monologue and the blame usually ends up on the chair. They whisper among themselves: 'Why didn't anyone step in? Why didn't the chair move on to the next agenda point? And why wasn't Mary asked for her opinion – after all, this is her project.' A good chair should prevent this from happening and take action during the meeting to ensure one person doesn't take up too much time.

Turn-yielding involves both taking turns to speak and allowing others to speak in conversations. It's vital that everyone has the opportunity to contribute. This skill requires being mindful of your own communication skills and ensuring that others have the chance to share their thoughts. However, some individuals lack self-awareness and tend to dominate conversations. As the facilitator, it's your responsibility to ensure everyone has an opportunity to speak. You can achieve this by interjecting when someone pauses or by summarizing their points and then redirecting the conversation to others. For example, you could say, 'So, to recap, Zayn, you mentioned that ABC is important. Douglas, what are your thoughts on that?'

Strategy 4: Be aware of time management

Determine beforehand how much time you truly need. I've seen many companies attempt to make complex decisions in a single meeting without allowing for adequate input gathering beforehand. Decisions can only be made with the right information, so ensure there's time for gathering input. Stick to the schedule and aim to keep meetings as concise as possible. Surprising people with shorter meetings than expected can be effective. If the default is to schedule an hour, try planning for just 30 minutes instead. You'll often find that people are more focused and productive in shorter, more condensed meetings. As the timekeeper, it's crucial to plan an assigned time for each agenda item accordingly. If it's more of a brainstorming session, be flexible and allow for creativity to flow without being constrained too much by time limits.

Strategy 5: Be mindful of emotions

In crisis situations with urgent deadlines, there are instances where we must temporarily set aside our emotions, prioritize the task at hand and address emotions afterwards. But essentially with any meeting you must deal with emotions first. When individuals are stressed or emotional, the cognitive part of the brain is compromised, making it difficult to focus, think clearly and stay calm.

This poses a real challenge to effective decision-making. Plus, stress messes with memory and how we process information, adding another layer of difficulty to making choices during a meeting. By checking in on everyone, acknowledging their input and paying attention to body language, you as the facilitator can quickly get everyone involved and on the same page.

I once suggested setting aside a brief 'complaining session' before starting the actual meeting because I picked up on a lot of emotions. We'd planned for a 45-minute meeting, but by the 25-minute mark, everyone was finished – they'd all expressed the same feelings and it was clear they needed to vent a bit. All the emotions stemmed from one key issue that was already on the agenda and airing it out relieved the tension. With that out of the way, they could tackle the agenda effectively.

Strategy 6: Be clear

I once supported a chair in becoming clearer and more direct in their communication. This person always used 12 sentences when one would suffice. This not only prolonged the meetings but also made it difficult for others to understand him. Unclear interventions create an unclear meeting. Be short and precise and make sure you are heard and know what you want from the people in the meeting. If you address people with a soft voice so no one can hear you, you are not a good conductor. If you let people talk all the time and don't intervene it's not effective. It's your role, you're responsible for creating an effective meeting so take that responsibility! Step up to the plate!

Strategy 7: Use the helicopter view

The helicopter metaphor describes an approach to how to look at meetings and navigate through them. The metaphor can be used to manage your skills as if you were a pilot in a helicopter who sees the entire landscape. It means observing all aspects of a situation to make informed decisions based on the bigger picture. In other words, examine the facts, behaviour and setting and conduct the meeting as needed. What that means is you listen carefully to what is said, how it's said and when it's said. You are the camera and pilot that can zoom in and out or focus on different aspects that are needed. You can start or stop the journey, get an overview, come back, land for a bit and take a break or stay on a topic, hovering for a while as we conduct the meeting from that helicopter view perspective.

Conclusion

With the right approach, meetings can be efficient, productive and maybe even enjoyable. As the chair, your awareness of the situation, commitment to your role and focus on key goals all set the tone and steer the outcome. Keep an eye on the time, practise turn-yielding and keep discussions on track. Respect everyone's input and avoid unnecessary detours. A well-run meeting doesn't just get things done, it also positively impacts your colleagues, strengthens the team and benefits the company as a whole. By focusing on clear objectives and creating a balanced, engaging atmosphere, every meeting becomes an opportunity to make progress, reach goals and build meaningful connections within the team.

CHAPTER TWENTY-FOUR

What to do if I want to be more approachable?

Saying 'My door is always open' might seem like a quick fix for managers feeling that they can deal with issues among their team members, but it's not always that simple. A troubling incident in the Netherlands saw 25 employees speaking out against a manager for bullying and creating an unsafe work environment. They all referred to it as a 'culture of fear'. The management's response was upsetting for some people. They emphasized that without people telling others about the culture of fear, things couldn't be resolved and that there would have been possibilities and procedures to address the behaviour at an earlier stage so things could have been prevented.

This caused a big outburst in the Dutch press and across the country. How could a leader be so ignorant as to think that mentioning that a door is open will lead to people addressing behaviour and giving feedback?

This really shows the problem when managers just rely on having procedures and being available without actually tackling the real issues of openness, respect and being approachable. There's often a big difference between having safety procedures in place and making sure people feel safe enough to actually use them. It's key to build a culture where people notice how others are treated and feel okay speaking up about it.

Managing is not sitting at a desk and hoping for people to come in when something is wrong. That's utopic. It's about connecting, interacting and communicating.

I once encountered a leader in charge of a company with 1,500 employees who were apprehensive about the management changes due to the retirement of their previous leader, with whom they had a strong rapport. Realizing the importance of building connections with such a large group, the new leader faced the challenge of how to effectively engage with everyone.

The leader decided to visit every team and department, presenting each member with an apple. This symbolic gesture not only introduced him face-to-face but also emphasized the idea of facing challenges head-on, focusing on the Dutch saying, 'You have to bite through the sour apple', which translates as something like, 'You have to swallow the bitter pill first'.

Interestingly, this wasn't just any company – it was actually my high school. The leader didn't just stop at the teachers and staff; he made sure to connect with all of us students, even though we weren't traditional 'employees'. By taking the time to personally connect with all of us, he laid a foundation of recognition and trust, which paid off later, even during tough conversations in his office with some of the students.

What really stuck with me was his nonverbal communication. He carried himself with a mix of humility and confidence. Even though some students initially made fun of him, standing there with a box full of apples, his approach of engaging with them directly, apple in hand, eventually turned their attitude into one of gratitude and respect. This experience underscores the power of genuine connection and nonverbal communication in leadership, demonstrating the impact of sincere gestures in fostering positive relationships within a large organization.

Here are some strategies you can use as a leader to connect.

Strategy 1: Be available

Actively making time to connect with your peers is crucial. Blocking out 30 minutes to an hour in your schedule might seem like a lot, but it's worth it. Whether it's loitering a bit near the coffee machine for a chat or actively calling an employee you haven't spoken to in a while, these small gestures can make a big difference.

A quick informal talk is also a great way to check in with someone and see how they're doing. It doesn't have to be an official meeting at all. And if you're working with a remote team, sending a few emails or making some calls can also help you stay connected. During coaching sessions with a manager overseeing a team of 80 employees, we identified that her span of control was exceeding manageable limits (Mindtools, n.d.). Typically, it's recommended that individuals reporting directly to you should be no more than 10 in total. The term 'span of control' first appeared in *The Soul and Body of an Army*, the 1921 book by Sir Ian Hamilton, a general in the British Army. He argued that military leaders became less effective as they had more people reporting directly to them. But circumstances sometimes dictate otherwise.

In this case some other managers were unable to work at that moment, leaving her to fill in the gaps and lead a team of 80 on top of her own responsibilities. To give her team more opportunities to connect with her, we added an extra hour each week where she was available, like a doctor's office hours. She informed her team that they could always reach out to her whenever needed, but this hour was specifically set aside for anyone who had unexpected issues or important updates to discuss. During this time, she was available to listen, provide guidance or address any concerns that arose, ensuring everyone felt supported. She also used this hour to proactively check in with team members, helping to strengthen communication and build stronger relationships within the team.

Strategy 2: Validate

Validation is all about recognizing, acknowledging and understanding others. It's key in communication and relationships because it builds trust and strengthens emotional connections. When people feel heard and valued, it boosts their emotional well-being and makes cooperation so much smoother. People don't just want to be part of a team; they want to feel like their contributions matter.

To be a more effective leader, start by regularly validating your team and colleagues. It's a small step that can make a huge difference in both morale and productivity. For example, you can thank them, give them positive feedback or actively listen when they are sharing information with you. For more specific tips, check out Chapter 21.

Strategy 3: Know your own leadership style and adapt

There's a sea of models out there that can help you figure out your leadership style. I'd suggest diving into as many books as you can on the topic. Don't worry if some seem a bit dated; they can still offer valuable insights that can prompt you to think about your own approach to leadership.

For starters, Hersey and Blanchard's take on situational leadership can show you how to adjust your style based on how ready and mature your employees are to perform tasks. Daniel Goleman talks about six leadership styles rooted in emotional intelligence. Douglas McGregor (1960) challenges you to consider how your perceptions of your employees shape your leadership. And Steve Radcliff's *Leadership: Plain and Simple* (2012) explores how your own drive and energy influence your leadership style. And that's just scratching the surface; there are countless more resources out there.

No matter what you read my advice is always the same. Use the information to reflect on yourself!

Ultimately, the two key questions are: Who am I, and who am I leading? Do my leadership style and my employees' needs align? For instance, if your team members thrive on independence, micromanaging them, even if you're detail-oriented, is not the best approach. As a leader, your main goal should be to make sure your employees feel comfortable and clearly understand their goals. When people feel supported and know what's expected of them, they're usually more motivated and productive.

Seeking feedback from others about your leadership style can give you valuable insights into how you're perceived as a leader. Ask for input on both your strengths and weaknesses. If you gather feedback directly from those you lead, you'll come to understand that your thoughts about your style may not always align with your actions.

For example, you may believe you're great at connecting with people, but if you're rarely available, that perception may not be accurate. It's important to understand that there can be a gap between your intentions and how your behaviour is perceived and feedback from your team can help close that gap. You could create a survey as a useful way to gather insights, allowing you to ask questions like, 'What do you see as my strengths and weaknesses as a leader?'

Strategy 4: Know your own body language and adapt

I worked with a young manager who was puzzled by feedback he got from his team describing him as intimidating. Unbeknownst to him, his loud voice was the cause; it was overwhelming enough that others felt like covering their ears. Changing this behaviour was challenging for him, as he had grown up in a large family where raising his voice was necessary to be heard. However, when he began altering his approach and speaking more softly in certain situations, he noticed an immediate impact. This change proved even more effective, as it introduced a different dynamic to the interactions.

Additionally, smiling can enhance your approachability, serving as a warm and welcoming gesture to initiate any conversation. Tilting your head slightly towards your shoulders communicates interest in what is being said. When combined with nodding during a conversation, it is often perceived as a sign that you encourage the person to continue speaking.

Furthermore, your torso plays a crucial role in effective communication. When engaging in a conversation, it's important to focus on the other person. Avoid remaining aligned with your computer; instead, turn your body towards them and ensure you pause what you are doing. If you need to take notes during the conversation, maintain eye contact as much as possible.

Also, be mindful of proximity. Many people tend to stand too close and this can be particularly important when hierarchy is involved. If you stand too close, especially in a workplace with hierarchical differences, it can make people feel uneasy or even threatened. By giving people a bit more space, it helps to make them feel more comfortable. If you maintain a respectful distance in professional settings, it shows that you're aware of personal boundaries and that you respect each individual's comfort level.

Strategy 5: Ask others how they want to be led by you

In my leadership trainings, I often assign participants a role-playing task where they pair up as leader and employee. This metaphorical exercise is designed to explore leading and following. However, it's rare for participants to begin by inquiring about their partner's leadership preferences or needs. This neglect typically results in the 'employee' feeling somewhat insecure and apprehensive, given the uncertainty of what to expect. As a result, many 'employees' feel unsure and hesitant, not knowing what the leader was planning or how they should respond. This leads to discussions afterwards, where 'employees' share that a simple question about their preferences could have made them feel more comfortable and confident. This exercise really highlights how easy it is to overlook communication about needs, even in situations where it could improve collaboration and trust. On the occasions where someone does take the time to understand their partner's preferences, the outcome is noticeably different: the employee appears more relaxed and cooperative. The reason? They are given a voice in the process.

Strategy 6: Give people room

Give your team the freedom to take charge, make their own decisions and share their ideas openly, without judgment or micromanagement. In cultures that value collaboration and equality, where everyone's input truly matters, this approach can be especially impactful.

For example, instead of jumping in with, 'Here's how we'll handle it', try saying, 'What are your thoughts on this approach?' or 'I trust your judgment – take the lead on this.' Simple shifts like these empower team members to explore their own methods, which builds their confidence and independence. It creates a workplace where they feel genuinely valued and respected, knowing that their contributions are both seen and trusted.

This openness invites them to come to you more freely with ideas, questions or concerns, fostering a strong sense of trust and connection. When you support them in finding their own way, you honour their personal preferences and development, while also creating a business culture that values individual responsibility, shared input and respect.

Strategy 7: What is your goal?

Whether your aim is to reduce costs, restructure an organization or build an efficient team to meet a tight deadline, being crystal clear about your goals as a manager is essential. When you openly share these objectives, you create a sense of transparency and clarity within the team, allowing everyone to understand the purpose behind their work.

This openness doesn't just provide direction, it also invites your team to approach you with questions, ideas or concerns directly tied to these goals, making them feel involved in the bigger picture. It helps create a culture of trust, where team members feel comfortable voicing their insights or flagging potential challenges before they become obstacles.

Remember: know your role, know your goal and bring your team along with you!

Conclusion

As a manager, it's crucial to make an active effort to connect with your team in meaningful ways. This can range from something as simple as a phone call to wish them a happy birthday to engaging in regular check-ins, where you genuinely listen to their ideas and concerns. If you want to build a connection, you should go beyond routine actions; it involves understanding your unique style and recognizing how it shapes your interactions. Knowing yourself, your strengths, weaknesses and communication preferences allows you to understand what to bring to each interaction.

To strengthen these connections further, ask your team members directly how they prefer to communicate and work. This can be especially important in culturally diverse teams, where acknowledging cultural norms and values is key.

Ultimately, being approachable starts with your willingness to reach out in ways that resonate with your team. Showing that you're culturally sensitive and open to different styles helps you build stronger, more trusting relationships that encourage openness and collaboration.

CHAPTER TWENTY-FIVE

What to do if people don't want to participate in a meeting?

If you've ever addressed a group as a manager, trainer or coach, you may have encountered disruptors at one point. These people show their disinterest in the meeting, for instance through nonverbal cues like sceptical looks and eye rolls or verbally by questioning your actions or explanations. They might show disruptive behaviours like whispering to someone nearby or making side comments during your talk. You could see small groups of two or three whispering, laughing or even speaking loudly, drawing attention away and interrupting your presentation.

It's not easy to be in front of a group; when you encounter certain behaviours you might feel distracted, annoyed or irritated. This behaviour isn't limited to presentations; it can also occur during meetings or training sessions and can distract you and create discomfort.

I once provided training for a team where one lady was showing reluctant behaviour from the moment she stepped into the room. I had never seen her before and she already showed hostility towards me when I shook her hand to introduce myself. With everything I said and asked she was grumpy, saying no and even showing eye-rolling behaviour.

Luckily this doesn't happen very often, but when it does, you as a teacher, manager or trainer have to act upon this behaviour or else the person will be a disruptive factor for not only you but for all the participants present.

Strategy 1: Relabelling

When Jacques van Harte (1951–2002) mentored me at the start of my career in the Netherlands in the 1990s, he emphasized the importance of observing behaviour, understanding its triggers for you personally and then reframing it. For instance, if someone is nagging, you should relabel it as someone with a keen critical eye. If they question your authority, it's an opportunity for you to showcase your knowledge. If they frequently disrupt with questions, it shows that they have an interest in what you're teaching. Even if someone is sleeping (as happened once in Jacques' training), it can be viewed positively as self-care and that you are able to create a relaxed atmosphere.

Bias towards behaviour comes into play because we all have automatic judgments or feelings about certain behaviours, often based on past experiences, cultural norms or personal preferences. Changing the way you label certain behaviours can help you let go of biases and emotional reactions toward them. This makes it easier to see things clearly and deal with the behaviour calmly and effectively.

Strategy 2: Make them your friend

Instead of criticizing someone for their behaviour, which may be your initial reaction, you can address them differently. If someone interrupts with something unrelated during your talk, try engaging them with a friendly question like, 'You seem to have an interesting perspective – how do you think this connects to what we're discussing?' This way, you're acknowledging their input while gently steering the conversation back. Or, if you want to keep things casual, you could say, 'You seem pretty knowledgeable – what are your thoughts on this?' This approach not only values their input but shows you're interested in their viewpoint as a friend, not just as a speaker. Validate their viewpoint by agreeing with something they say. This way, you're inviting them to contribute and share their knowledge to benefit others. When they're engaged instead of disconnected, it can add an extra dimension to the training.

Strategy 3: Ignore

Sometimes, the best course of action is to choose not to act immediately. This approach is referred to as 'strategic inaction'. It involves consciously deciding to do nothing in response to a situation. This is particularly useful when you are dealing with behaviours that seek to provoke a reaction.

Sometimes, the most effective response is simply to do nothing. By holding back, you're not giving the person the reaction they're looking for, signalling that their approach isn't working. This can subtly encourage them to shift their tactics. Also, strategic inaction gives you time to assess the situation more thoroughly. It allows you to observe and gather more information before deciding what the most appropriate response should be. This can be particularly beneficial in complex scenarios where the motivations behind a behaviour are not immediately clear, or where intervening could escalate the situation unnecessarily.

I remember a participant who kept mumbling comments during a session. I couldn't quite catch what he was saying and it was a bit distracting at first. But after about 10 minutes, it stopped and he became fully engaged in the training. Sometimes, you just need to give people a little time to settle in or let them do what they need to do before they can commit to being there.

Strategy 4: Reward behaviour of others or set an example

It's rare to find an entire group against you. Focus on those who are engaged. If you praise and highlight positive behaviour it often encourages others to join in. You might say something like, 'I really appreciate how everyone here is jumping in and sharing ideas – it's making this session so much more dynamic!' By highlighting and praising the positive behaviour, you create a ripple effect. The ones hanging back might not want to feel left out, especially when they see their colleagues getting into it and enjoying the activities or discussions. Often, they'll start to match the energy and enthusiasm of the group, wanting to be part of the fun and learning too.

Strategy 5: Ask questions

You can make a lot of assumptions about someone's behaviour, but to truly understand what's happening, just ask! Start by describing the observed behaviour and inquire about what might be going on. You could start by mentioning what you've noticed, like, 'I see you've been on your phone quite a bit. Is everything alright?' This opens the door for them to share. For instance, there was this one time I noticed someone constantly checking their phone and she seemed distracted. When I asked, she apologized and explained that she was waiting for a call from her realtor to find out if her offer on a house was accepted. It made total sense why she was so preoccupied!

Strategy 6: Be vulnerable and honest

Being vulnerable involves acknowledging your own uncertainties and insecurities, such as by asking, 'Am I doing something wrong?' For example, you can express vulnerability by sharing the impact of someone's behaviour on you, as in, 'I've just presented my approach to this project and now I see you laughing. This makes me feel awkward and it is like you're making fun of my approach. I hope that's not the case?'

Additionally, asking if you should change something might help. I once encountered a situation where someone seemed very disconnected, so I asked, 'Is there anything I can do with my teaching approach to help you re-engage?' They explained that they just needed some fresh air and that a short break would be much appreciated. Opening up like this can lead to more genuine communication and create a sense of comfort for everyone involved. After the break, everyone returned with a fresh focus.

Strategy 7: Explain the effect

Sometimes individuals aren't aware of how their actions ripple through a room, affecting the atmosphere and the conversation. They might be so focused on their own viewpoint that they overlook the impact they have on others. For example, it could be that someone repeatedly speaks over others because they're enthusiastic or used to fast-paced conversations, not realizing that others find it interruptive. Or they might be checking their phone, thinking they're multitasking, unaware that it appears as if they're disengaged. These small behaviours might not be intended to bother others but can create frustration or disrupt the team dynamic.

As a leader or colleague, it might be challenging to address disruptive behaviours. Many people assume these disruptions are intentional, without realizing that often, they're just unconscious habits or actions, without considering their impact on others. By helping the person displaying the behaviour understand how their actions affect the team, you give them a chance to see things from a fresh perspective and make more mindful choices.

By gently pointing out how these actions affect you, the team or the setting, you're helping them become aware of these unconscious habits, giving them a chance to adjust in a way that supports the meeting. This approach is about bringing possible unconscious behaviours into awareness, making it easier for the person to shift to more positive and supportive actions. It isn't just about raising awareness; it's about empowering everyone to actively contribute to a positive team dynamic.

An example could be, 'I don't know if you are aware of the fact that you are chatting throughout the presentation. It's distracting me and I'm concerned you might be missing important information about this project. Could you please listen to the presentation first, before commenting?'

Conclusion

I chose to utilize the last three strategies during the team training session, focusing on that hesitant lady's participation. I told her my observations, the effect and was vulnerable: 'Hey Barbara, I hear you commenting on the side about what I'm presenting. This is a bit distracting to me. Is there anything that I'm doing wrong according to you?'

She replied, 'No, it's not you personally. I'm just not in the mood for yet another training session on communication skills.'

I answered, 'Well I can fully understand that if you have had multiple training sessions already, this one might be one too many. But then let's do the following: if you don't want to be here, don't be here. Because it's exhausting for you to have to endure this, but, also, it's not nice for me to feel your negativity when you are mumbling all the time. I feel uncomfortable when you do that and I would like to feel comfortable.'

The best part was that, from that moment on, she straightened up and engaged in the training. Later, she thanked me, saying it was unlike any training she'd had before, she actually enjoyed it and felt she'd taken away some real, valuable insights.

CHAPTER TWENTY-SIX

What to do if people don't do what they are supposed to do?

It's more common than you might think: people not meeting job expectations. I discussed this back in Chapter 19. But what if you're the leader dealing with it? Managers often feel significant frustration when team members fall short, facing all kinds of challenges – employees showing up late, failing to follow through on promises, not communicating well or simply not being a good fit for the role.

When discussing this with American colleagues, they're often taken aback, suggesting, 'Why not just fire them?' However, in Europe, the situation is a bit more complex due to strong labour protections. Employers are required to create a supportive work environment and, if an employee is struggling with issues – be it mentally, physically or in relation to their tasks – they must offer extensive assistance to improve their situation or help them get back on track.

It's crucial to address someone who isn't performing well in their job. However, when we discuss the fact that someone is not doing their job it's about balancing accountability with compassion, recognizing the broader legal and cultural context.

Here are some strategies to help you.

Strategy 1: Hire the right one

Hiring the right person for the job seems like common sense but finding that perfect fit isn't always easy. Sometimes, you might find someone who still needs to learn certain aspects of the role and that's okay. If you have the time and energy to guide them, it could be a great way to fill the vacancy. Just be sure the gap in skills or experience isn't too large to bridge.

If you're limited on time or have no budget for training, it's unrealistic to expect someone to meet all your expectations without support. Growth requires resources, and if they're not available, it's hard for anyone to magically develop the skills and knowledge needed to excel in a new or challenging role. Their experience and training opportunities need to align with your expectations.

Similarly, while someone's friendly or positive personality can be a great asset, it doesn't necessarily mean they have the specific skills needed for the job. Being nice or easy-going is valuable in a team setting, but it doesn't guarantee competence or the ability to handle complex tasks. Friendly personalities don't replace the need for technical knowledge, analytical skills or project management capabilities.

A resume or charming personality can seem impressive, but hiring mistakes are often made at the very start of filling a vacancy. Just because a candidate is friendly or already well-liked within the company doesn't mean they'll deliver the results you need. Focus on the concrete skills and behaviours they bring to the role, rather than relying solely on personality. Do your due diligence! Check their CV, follow up on the recommendations, check them online, ask others about their interactions with this person and work with assessments during the interview trajectory so you can actually check their behavioural skills. They might dazzle you in an interview, but you need to see beyond that moment in time. What is their history and how did they interact in their previous job? To get beyond a dazzling resume or charming personality, consider asking a question like, 'Can you share a time when you faced a challenging project and describe the specific steps you took to deliver results? What did you learn about your working style from that experience?' or 'Can you describe a time when your natural approach or personality led to a difficulty or misunderstanding at work? How did you handle it, and what did you learn from the experience?' This all gives insight into not only the content but also how people handle those questions.

My favourite question to ask in a job interview is, 'What's the best experience you've had in life so far, and why?' This question offers valuable insight into a candidate's values, experiences and how passionate they can be. Of course, you should ask plenty of other questions, but this one is a great icebreaker to start the conversation.

Keep in mind that being personable or enthusiastic doesn't guarantee strong performance in a role. As we've said, niceness doesn't always mean effectiveness or genuine kindness; it's essential to focus on actual behaviour, interaction and skills. Aligning your expectations with a person's capabilities and the resources available can prevent frustrations later, for both you and the employee. I'll touch more on preventing hiring toxic personalities in the final part of the book, but for now, remember that some people can be surprisingly convincing at first glance. Be sure to do your due diligence!

Strategy 2: Find out why they are failing

Asking why someone isn't completing tasks or fulfilling their duties gives you insight into the reasons why. You get a chance to discover if you can assist them or if the situation is beyond help. It gives you the opportunity to determine whether the challenges they're facing are within your capacity to assist or if they require external support. Sometimes, the reasons may be personal, such as health issues or family concerns. Other times, it may be a lack of knowledge or skills preventing them from completing tasks effectively, in which case targeted training or guidance could be provided to fix it. You could ask, 'Can you walk me through the main challenges you're facing with your current tasks? Understanding what's holding you back will help us figure out if there are ways I can support you, or if we need to look into other types of assistance or resources.'

Strategy 3: Provide training

When an employee lacks the necessary skills or knowledge for their role, it's usually worth investing extra time and resources into training. By doing so, a company not only supports its people but also gives them the opportunity to learn and grow. Yes, it takes both time and money, but replacing an employee is often much more expensive and time-consuming than helping a current one develop.

Employees can expand their knowledge through online courses or manuals – great tools for technical learning. However, developing soft skills is just as important for their overall growth. As someone who regularly teaches these skills, I can't emphasize enough how crucial they are, especially for managers. While I always recommend live, in-person training over online learning, any form of training is better than none. Dedicating time to soft skills like communication and leadership allows managers to build stronger relationships with their teams, improve performance and become more effective leaders.

I know of a situation where someone was fired for not displaying certain behaviours, but the issue was that no one ever gave them specific feedback or a chance to improve. Even during performance reviews, everything was positive – no mention of any areas for growth. Because of the lack of clear feedback and documentation, this nearly ended up in a court case. Ultimately, the company settled because the case wouldn't have stood a chance in court.

If you don't give employees the opportunity to learn and grow, I believe the company has failed in its responsibility.

Strategy 4: Provide coaching

Unlike training, where you typically work in a group and benefit from learning alongside others, one-on-one coaching offers a personalized approach that can truly make a difference for someone. It's all about individual attention, helping someone change their thoughts, beliefs and behaviours. When an employee recognizes they're not doing what needs to be done and is ready to make a change, coaching gives them the support they need. Working with a behavioural expert, for example, means getting specific strategies and guidance to help them adapt their behaviour and achieve their goals.

I had the opportunity to work closely with a board member who was very open to letting me observe him in meetings and collaborate directly to improve his effectiveness. After just three sessions, we wrapped up because the personalized coaching was so impactful and precisely targeted to his needs. Working on these high-performance trajectories is one of my favourite parts of my job. It's incredibly rewarding to see how a tailored, individual approach can give someone a significant boost in their behaviour and performance.

Strategy 5: Address consequences

People should know that if they are lacking in their job it has consequences. In 1999, NASA lost their Mars Climate Orbiter spacecraft due to a navigation error caused by a mix-up between metric and imperial units. This simple oversight led to the failure of the mission, resulting in a loss of around $125 million (Lee Hotz, 1999).

If you don't address inefficiency or failure, the consequences can be big. It could be financially, socially or even in terms of reputation. Underperformance in any form can seriously harm a company. If an employee is not meeting expectations (like missing deadlines or making mistakes), it makes both colleagues and clients question whether the company can deliver quality work and maintain professionalism. This is an issue that affects the company's reputation and trust. For example, imagine a team member who consistently misses deadlines or delivers bad work. Not only does that slow down the entire project, but it can affect the whole team's morale or upset a client and ultimately cost the company money.

When employees don't understand how their role contributes to the bigger picture, they might start seeing their tasks as unimportant or irrelevant. This perception can contribute to underperformance, because if they don't feel their work matters, they may lack the motivation to perform well. Clients may start to question whether the company can deliver quality work on time or maintain a professional and reliable environment. Whether it's the CEO or a factory worker, failing to meet expectations can have a costly impact.

This is where recognition and validation play a role (Navarro and Oud, 2021). When employees feel valued and understand how their work contributes to the company's success, they are more motivated and aligned with the company's goals. That's why validation is so important; without it, employees might feel their work is unimportant, leading to disengagement and further underperformance (see Chapter 24 on validation).

Strategy 6: Use rewards and disciplining

Offering a little extra incentive can sometimes make a big difference, even though people are already paid to do their job. You could think of handing out a bonus or a special reward to encourage the team to give that extra push. I remember this one time with a team on the brink of giving up on a project. They were running on empty, ready to throw in the towel after pushing themselves so hard. But the promise of an extended weekend off was just the boost they needed to cross the finish line. It's amazing how a small gesture can turn the tide and re-energize an entire team. Unexpected rewards give a boost of dopamine and can just give that extra needed nudge.

The opposite would be penalizing a team. For instance, instead of offering bonuses or incentives for achieving sales goals, the company starts penalizing the team by reducing their commissions or imposing fines for missing targets. For some individuals or teams, the threat of a penalty can be a strong motivator to correct behaviour or improve performance to avoid negative consequences. If we don't finish this as planned, we won't be able to get that next project.

I'm not a fan of punishing since it rarely motivates people to get the right behaviour in order. But with an undisciplined team it might sometimes help to show how serious certain consequences can be if they are not focused on specific goals.

Strategy 7: Be decisive

Sometimes it's crystal clear: you must let people go. Yes, it involves costs for recruiting, hiring and training new candidates, or maybe even the cost of a court case, but it can turn out to be a smart and inevitable move because there is ineffectiveness or even people who are damaging the company.

However, it's important to note that the process differs significantly between Europe, the UK and the US. I won't go into all the details of each country. In some countries the risk of an unfair dismissal claim can be more difficult than in other countries. Terminating in the UK is a long process and a lot of information needs to be provided before you can take steps to let someone go.

For example, in the Netherlands, dismissal is a complex process due to strict labour laws emphasizing employee rights. It requires a valid basis and procedural adherence for dismissal. This often leads to employees being shuffled between departments instead of being let go. It's crucial to recognize when it's necessary to dismiss someone for the team's safety, the company's benefit and other reasons. Allowing the situation to fester can only lead to bigger problems. Despite the hurdles, it's important to address the situation directly and firmly when 'enough is enough'. Taking a stand as a company to let some people go (even when it costs money) might be a good decision for morale, setting an example and creating safety.

In some companies I've worked for, I've overheard people say, 'It doesn't matter what kind of odd behaviour someone shows here, they'll never get fired anyway.' This mindset breeds frustration and resentment among those who are putting in the effort. When employees sense that certain individuals can get away with poor behaviour without facing any consequences, it demotivates those who are working hard. It creates the question: if others can slack off with no repercussions, why should I bother giving my best? This kind of attitude can be harmful, leading to a culture of disengagement and indifference. As a leader, it's your responsibility to address this behaviour head-on and make tough decisions to prevent this from happening.

Conclusion

Don't underestimate the importance of addressing the situation when someone is falling short of meeting their job requirements. It's vital to listen to feedback from colleagues, clients and your own observations. While it's your role to offer support, it's also important to recognize your limits as a manager; there's only so much you can do. Being proactive and paying attention to the signs is essential so you can take the right steps to address the issue. Ignoring it will only let negativity fester, so it's essential to step in and set clear expectations. Holding everyone accountable creates an environment where hard work is valued, helping to maintain motivation and a positive team dynamic. Whether that means investing in the colleague's development, offering additional support or ultimately deciding to part ways, taking action is key.

CHAPTER TWENTY-SEVEN

What to do if I want to become a more trustworthy leader?

A lot has been written about charismatic leadership – wonderful leaders like Martin Luther King, Franklin D. Roosevelt and Nelson Mandela. But what if you want to become one? Not as a leader of millions of followers, but just to be there as a great and trustworthy leader for your team. You as a beacon of calm, trust and knowledge, amidst all the turmoil in an organization.

I've been fortunate to be trained by some of the best trainers, mentors and teachers in the world, and I've met great leaders within various companies. This was true even when I was an employee before founding The Behaviour Company. What stood out most was their trust in me and their invaluable guidance.

One of my experiences with great leadership was in my first job, right after I finished at the University of Applied Sciences and started working with one of my first groups. I encountered a negative situation where a group of participants were very dismissive and I even received some inappropriate, sexually charged remarks. Being young and inexperienced, I felt intimidated by the group and didn't know how to respond.

Afterwards I was sitting in my car crying and I called my boss. It was a two-day training session and I had no intention whatsoever of going back the next day. His remark: 'You must. I don't care what you do. I've got your back no matter what. But you must be in front of that group and not bail.'

But the best part was that he said, 'And I promise you this, if you do this, it will strengthen you for the rest of your life. It will give you confidence and you will never forget it.'

He was right. Not only did I go back to that group, I was also able, as best as it went, to make an intervention and address my discomfort in that group and their behaviour.

My boss believed in me and that gave me a certain power to do what I needed to do.

You might not be a world-class leader yet, but certain strategies can help you become the boss your team needs.

Strategy 1: Show your trustworthiness

As a leader, you want to be worthy of trust. To get things done and build connections with others, you need to act consistently and transparently, making others feel confident that you will do what you say and act in their best interest. It's essential to show your trustworthiness through your behaviour, because how you act often speaks louder than what you say.

One thing I always emphasize in my teaching is the importance of showing trustworthiness through your behaviour, not just relying on words or interactions. Pay attention to your body language, tone of voice and other nonverbal cues, as these are key to demonstrating your intentions and reliability. Actions, tone, posture, proximity and gestures all play a role in conveying your message and revealing your true character. Trust is built through consistent, positive behaviour, so make sure your actions align with your words.

For example, if you say you'll send an email, make sure you actually do it. If you promise to think about something, take the time to genuinely consider it. Your body language can reinforce this: maintaining eye contact when making promises, nodding in agreement and using open, relaxed gestures all signal that you're present and sincere. Too often, managers say yes or make promises just to wrap up a conversation quickly because they're busy. While this might seem efficient in the moment, it can damage trust in the long run, especially if your body language says otherwise – like avoiding eye contact or being distracted by your phone.

Strategy 2: Use validation

In my experience, validation is a trait a leader should practice daily. As a manager, your role isn't just about managing objectives, it's also about managing people. This means you have to listen, make time for your team and understand that they need your attention and validation. It's one of the easiest things to improve in business, yet it's often overlooked.

One of my clients was working double-time because her colleague got sick; she was homeschooling two children, living in a small apartment and trying to do everything to help the company. She didn't mind being flexible, she didn't mind working hard and working longer hours; what she minded was that there was a lack of acknowledgement on the part of her manager: 'The only thing I wished for was that once the manager would have said thank you for being so flexible, for taking on this added burden.'

Express gratitude regularly for others' efforts and contributions. I once worked with someone whose manager took credit for his idea, leaving him feeling unappreciated. As a manager, it's important to express gratitude and give credit where it's due. A simple thank you can make a big difference, building trust and fostering a positive, collaborative environment. It's a simple way to show you value your team.

Validation isn't just about hearing someone describing a situation and listening. It's about really acknowledging what they're saying and figuring out what they need to move forward. Managers need to get good at noticing and understanding their team's needs and concerns and then acting upon them.

Strategy 3: Be time-conscious

You can enhance your trustworthiness through time-conscious actions. Trust is built on respect and respecting your team's time is a critical aspect of this. Be punctual for meetings and stick to the agreed-upon schedule. When setting deadlines, make sure they are realistic and considerate of everyone's workload. By managing time well, you demonstrate reliability and show that you value the time of others.

I heard of a manager who continuously postponed meetings. The employee affected by this grew more anxious with each delay. She wanted to discuss some concerns she had already mentioned in an email, hoping to address certain important topics. The repeated postponements gave her the impression that the manager didn't want to address these issues at all. Even after she pointed out that it was urgent and affecting her health, the manager continued to postpone. This was devastating for her. Don't be like this manager.

Strategy 4: Follow up

Following up on commitments is essential in maintaining trust. If you promise to send an email, provide feedback or check in on a project, make sure you do it. Even if there's no update, it's helpful to let the team know there's nothing new to report – this way, people won't feel like you've forgotten about them or the task at hand.

I remember a story about a manager who was asked to handle an important task. He worked on it diligently but failed to update his colleague about his progress. She was left in the dark, thinking he hadn't done anything and when she eventually found out, she was frustrated and angry with him. The lack of communication had created unnecessary tension, even though the manager was working hard on the task.

It's also important to follow up on personal interactions, like checking in with a team member who mentioned they were struggling with a task. For example, if someone is returning to work after being sick for a while, take the time to check in every now and then to see how they're adjusting. These small acts of communication can go a long way in building trust.

Strategy 5: Make sure you are likeable

Some people might like you more than others, but there are things you can do to become a more likable leader. One important factor in being seen as trustworthy is having good manners. We can discuss what good manners mean to you specifically, but it has a lot to do with respect, kindness and consideration.

In this chapter, when I refer to good manners, I'm talking about those everyday actions that show respect and thoughtfulness toward others; for instance, if someone drops something, offering to pick it up, or if someone's hands are full, holding the door or helping them carry their items. This isn't about doing someone else's work for them – it's about being proactive and considerate. Good manners also involve things like not interrupting, listening attentively and simply being kind.

To become more likable, focus on smiling, making eye contact and being open to have conversations. Listen actively by paying attention, showing interest and responding thoughtfully.

I'll admit, I'm not the best with names, but I always try to connect with people in other ways. I try to remember something personal about them, like the fact that they have a dog or recently went on vacation. It's not about remembering every detail but showing a genuine interest in their lives. Asking about things they've mentioned in passing or recalling something from a previous conversation makes people feel valued. It's this small effort to connect on a personal level that helps build rapport and trust, which goes a long way in creating stronger relationships.

Giving credit where credit is due, rather than taking all the credit for team successes, plays a big role in being likable because it shows humility and appreciation for others' contributions. When you acknowledge the hard work of those around you, it fosters a sense of respect and teamwork, which people genuinely appreciate.

Lastly, offer assistance and support without expecting anything in return, as acts of kindness significantly boost likability. People appreciate when you're genuinely helpful and it creates a positive environment where others feel comfortable reaching out. For example, a manager once helped an employee move house on the weekend, knowing they were stressed. This kind gesture built trust and made the employee feel valued, both personally and professionally.

Strategy 6: Training self-enhancement

Are you demonstrating a willingness to learn, improve yourself, seek feedback and train to become better? Books, training sessions and feedback will help you improve. I'm fortunate to work with charismatic and eager leaders who are dedicated to self-improvement and want to learn more. They often ask questions like, 'How can I improve my body language?' 'How can I communicate more clearly?' and 'What can I do to better support my team?' These leaders recognize that learning doesn't stop when they reach a high position in the company. They are committed to continuous improvement, which to me is the essence of true leadership.

Strategy 7: Showing credibility

Credibility means that team members trust your judgment and integrity and believe that you as the leader have the knowledge and skills to guide the team effectively. When you as a manager make informed decisions and can clearly explain the reasoning behind them, your credibility grows. This transparency helps build trust, as the team can see that decisions are made based on solid knowledge, not guesswork.

For example, a manager I know had to make a difficult decision about reassigning responsibilities within the team. She took the time to explain her reasoning – based on each team member's strengths, the needs of the project and feedback from others. Afterwards, the team understood her decision, which helped strengthen their trust in her leadership.

Conclusion

To show trustworthiness, you must be honest and transparent in your communication. Follow through on your commitments and promises consistently, so your team can rely on you. It's important to treat everyone with respect and fairness, ensuring that all team members feel valued. Your actions must align with your words. Don't just talk about values like integrity, but actively demonstrate them in how you lead and interact with others.

Being knowledgeable and reliable is key, but it's also important to regularly assess whether your actions are having the desired effect. Showing trustworthiness means you're not just telling your team what to do but also leading by example and making sure your behaviour reflects the trust they place in you.

CHAPTER TWENTY-EIGHT

What to do if you're leading a diverse team with different needs, preferences and cultural backgrounds?

As leaders we need to understand that people come from different backgrounds, that they have different personalities and different experiences that shape their preferences in our leadership style.

While you don't have to constantly change your core leadership identity like a chameleon, being aware that no single style works for all situations and individuals is key. Different situations call for different leadership styles. For instance, during a crisis, a more directive approach might be necessary to make quick decisions and provide clear instructions. Contrarily, in a creative brainstorming session, a more participative and open style could encourage innovation and collaboration.

Time and place aren't the only things that shape your strategy; your team will have different needs and expectations too. How do you handle different cultures, styles and needs? How can you address the whole team while still considering everyone's unique differences? It's important not to fall into the trap of treating everyone the same. Recognizing and valuing differences makes for a more inclusive and effective team.

I once heard a story about a young woman who had just started her first job. Her boss expected quick action and high performance right from the start. However, he didn't give her the time or guidance needed to adjust to her new role. Having been used to working with an established, highly effective team, he didn't recognize that his leadership style needed to be adjusted for a new, less experienced team member. As a result, the woman felt overwhelmed and unsupported, struggling to meet expectations without proper onboarding or guidance. Adapting leadership styles to fit the needs of each individual team member is very important, especially when someone is new to the role.

As a team leader, adjusting your approach to meet individual needs is crucial to create a more harmonious and productive work environment. Here are some strategies to consider.

Strategy 1: Recognize the variety of differences among people

Observe the differences around you, such as generational, cultural and personal style variations.

Different generations have different expectations and preferences for leadership. For example, younger generations might prefer leaders who emphasize work-life balance and social responsibility, while older generations might value traditional leadership traits such as authority and experience. Books like *Generations*, by Jean M. Twenge (2023) can help you learn more about the different generations. While it doesn't cover Generation Alpha (born from 2010 to 2024), it still provides valuable insights into generational differences and dynamics from the generations before that.

Personality traits also play a role in leadership preferences. Someone who values structure and order might prefer an authoritative leader, while someone who values creativity and autonomy might lean towards a more democratic or laissez-faire leader.

Cultural differences are also significant. How people view hierarchy or speak up in meetings can vary a lot depending on the culture. One of the best books on this topic is *The Culture Map* by Erin Meyer (2014), which gives helpful insights into the challenges and rewards of working with people from different cultures.

Learning and working styles play a big role in leadership preferences. Some people need hands-on guidance, while others work best with independence. I once worked with a manager who tailored her approach based on these differences. One team member loved structure, so she gave her detailed daily checklists. Another preferred autonomy, so she set broad goals and checked in only occasionally. By adjusting to each person's style, she got the best out of everyone, fostering both productivity and job satisfaction.

Also, values and beliefs play a significant role in shaping what individuals consider good leadership. People's core values, such as integrity, honesty or fairness, often determine what they expect from their leaders.

In addition to values, health, ability and overall well-being also influence how leadership is perceived and what support is needed. For instance, an employee dealing with a disability or chronic fatigue might need more flexibility, such as adjusting work hours or providing additional support, to perform at their best.

Strategy 2: Encourage open communication

Create an environment where team members feel safe and comfortable sharing their thoughts, concerns and preferences. Encourage open conversations where individuals from diverse cultures and backgrounds can share their experiences and perspectives. This helps challenge stereotypes and build mutual respect. A great way to promote understanding is by inviting team members to create a presentation with their views on leadership based on their culture or country and how they personally relate to those perspectives. 'What is a good leader according to you and why? Or what is great team cooperation and why?' This can spark a team discussion about common values, shared goals and different approaches, ultimately strengthening the team's cohesion and collaboration. Ask them to share their opinions and observe the nonverbal communication to see if they are willing to interact with each other on a basis of equality. Pay close attention to the interaction and make sure you address any signs of disrespect, discomfort or disengagement promptly.

Sometimes it's advisable for a leader to step back, especially when hierarchy plays a significant role. Create safe spaces where team members can discuss sensitive issues openly. This might include you not being there, using anonymous feedback channels, written communication instead of face-to-face conversations or organizing smaller discussion groups where people feel more comfortable sharing their thoughts.

To align with all needs, you as a leader should use a balanced communication style. Using a mix shows that you value all team members' input and respect their preferences.

Strategy 3: Promote collaboration

When you have a diverse team, see it as an opportunity to learn from each other and enhance decision-making by looking at problems from different angles. Building diverse teams with people from various cultures and backgrounds can enhance creativity and problem-solving by bringing different viewpoints and approaches to the table.

You can create mentorship programmes where individuals from different cultures and backgrounds can learn from each other's experiences. Peer learning groups can be effective for sharing best practices and insights, further strengthening the team's overall capability. For example, one team member can give a brief insight into a work-related value from their cultural background such as how feedback is approached or how hierarchy is perceived. Encourage team members to collaborate and share their unique approaches.

At one company I worked with, a tech team hired an artist for a project to encourage creative thinking and bring fresh perspectives to the table. While not every idea was directly applicable, the artist's approach inspired the team to see the problem in a whole new light, helping them think outside the box.

Strategy 4: Set clear goals and expectations

While making room for different approaches, it's key to set clear goals and expectations for the team. Make sure everyone knows the common objectives and their role in hitting them.

You can give team members flexibility in how they tackle their tasks, as long as it fits with the context, work structure and company policies. While the focus and goals remain clear, the approach can vary – this could mean offering flexible working hours, allowing individuals to choose their methods, or providing the option to work remotely.

Encourage open discussions about team members' preferences to support their unique needs while keeping everyone on track. If you focus on the goals with flexibility, you create a more inclusive, efficient and motivated team. It's also important to explain your decisions and the reasons behind certain rules to ensure transparency because it helps prevent feelings of jealousy or exclusion.

Strategy 5: Provide a supportive, diverse environment

Provide support and mediation when necessary to maintain a positive and cooperative team atmosphere. Additionally, offering training sessions and resources, and sometimes even mediation tailored to the diverse needs of your team, can be very helpful. These sessions could focus on communication techniques, interpersonal skills or specific themed workshops. You can educate team members about cultural differences and promote understanding and respect.

It's important to actively address tensions that come from different ways of working. When something comes up, don't ignore it. Step in early and offer support to keep the atmosphere open and constructive. This could mean a brief one-on-one, a reset in a team meeting or a targeted session on communication or collaboration.

Helping your team to have respectful and diversity-focused discussions will go a long way in creating and maintaining an inclusive and diverse environment. You can get them engaged in activities and conversations that focus on understanding different perspectives, practising active listening and learning how to navigate and discuss sensitive topics respectfully.

After Covid, many people didn't want to return to the office after experiencing the benefits of remote work. A team I worked with found a middle ground by reducing the required office time at the main location. They came to an understanding where they allowed team members to work from home but required them to come into the office once a week and for special occasions. Additionally, they held monthly check-ins to see if this arrangement was causing any issues or needed adjustments. In the end, it worked out really well.

Strategy 6: Ensuring inclusivity in communication and activities

It's important to ensure that all forms of communication and activities are inclusive. For example, if your team includes members with hearing impairments, incorporate more written communication or learn sign language.

Utilize charts, diagrams and other aids to help communicate your points clearly. Visuals can help bridge the gap between different communication preferences. Another idea could be to provide translation services or multilingual materials for team members who are not fluent in the primary language used. For team members with visual impairments, think about using screen readers and providing documents in braille or large print. You can also offer flexible work arrangements and create quiet workspaces to meet different sensory needs.

And always consider accessibility when planning events or meetings.

I recall an incident at a team outing with a company where they completely overlooked that one of the employees was in a wheelchair and couldn't access the beach. It's hard to believe that such an important detail was forgotten, especially when a simple solution, like renting a beach wheelchair, was available. This oversight shows how crucial inclusive thinking and planning are. It's a stark reminder that being mindful of everyone's needs is essential to creating a truly inclusive and effective team environment.

Strategy 7: Celebrate cultural celebrations and events

Hosting cultural events and celebrations can educate participants about different traditions, practices and values, promoting inclusivity and understanding.

One of my favourite assignments for global teams is to bring a dish from their home country to the training session. During lunch, we enjoy a fuddle or a potluck with a variety of delicious foods from different regions around the world, ranging from warm to cold, from sweet to spicy.

What makes the meal even more special is when I ask each participant to share the story behind their dish. They might talk about how the recipe has been passed down through generations in their family or how they bought the ingredients from their favourite local market – maybe even one owned by a relative. These personal stories help us connect more deeply with each other. Sharing food in this way strengthens our bonds and creates a sense of unity.

Conclusion

To lead a diverse team with different needs, preferences and cultural backgrounds, it's important to be adaptable and responsive. Take time to understand each team member's unique needs, whether related to communication, work style or cultural expectations. You can achieve this through open conversations, regular feedback and observation.

Being culturally aware and flexible is key to avoiding misunderstandings and fostering inclusivity. Adapting to these needs helps create an environment where everyone feels valued, which in turn boosts collaboration and team effectiveness.

By tailoring your leadership approach, you can build stronger relationships and be a more respected, effective leader.

PART FIVE

Difficult situations

Difficult situations happen every day, but with some effort we have the chance to make them less challenging. It's normal to feel uncomfortable when someone becomes emotional, but whether they're crying or angry, these are just emotions and we shouldn't be afraid of them. However, things become more challenging when you're talking to someone who doesn't consider the feelings of others, is dismissive, careless or overly emotional themselves. In these cases, the conversation can become even harder to navigate.

Someone once asked me, 'What makes a situation difficult? What defines a difficult person?' For me, it all ties back to the three principles I shared earlier in this book. *If you're unable to create a sense of comfort, if you're unaware of your role and goal, and if you can't observe and respond appropriately to what the conversation requires, you may find yourself in challenging situations.* In fact, you might even become the difficult person in the room, leading to more tough conversations than necessary.

These difficult situations can escalate quickly and lead to misunderstandings and frustration on both sides. However, by being mindful of the core principles – 'creating comfort, understanding your role and goal and being observant to the needs of the conversation' and using the Helicopter Metaphor Technique – you can navigate challenging scenarios with greater ease. It's about taking responsibility for your part in the conversation and striving to create a more constructive dialogue, regardless of the circumstances or the person you're dealing with. It doesn't mean there will always be a positive outcome. Sometimes, it means you must recognize when it's necessary to end the conversation, establish boundaries or even walk away.

CHAPTER TWENTY-NINE

What to do if someone is crying?

Crying is a significant form of nonverbal communication. It signals to others that we are experiencing distress or need support, often creating empathy and assistance from those around us. While crying in a professional setting might feel uncomfortable, it's important to recognize that it is a natural human response and a healthy way of expressing emotions. Whether it's sadness, stress or even happiness, crying allows us to release our feelings. It's simply another form of communication that shows how someone feels in that moment. So, when someone starts crying during a meeting or conversation, there's no need to feel awkward or surprised. It's a sign of vulnerability, and responding with empathy can create a more supportive and understanding environment.

People often tell me how embarrassed they feel when others see them crying and just the thought of it is daunting to them. They tend to rather hide their emotions when tears start to well up, especially in front of clients or their boss, as it can be perceived as negative and unprofessional. This discomfort is often rooted in a sense of diminishing their power and status. People feel embarrassed because they aspire to be seen as strong and capable, as an individual being able to manage life's challenges and emotions and they feel crying is not portraying that.

As colleagues or leaders, it's up to us to help them feel less uncomfortable in these moments. By responding with empathy and understanding, we can create a supportive atmosphere that allows the individual to feel safe expressing their emotions. Acknowledging their vulnerability with kindness can help reduce the stigma surrounding tears and help them feel more at ease, ensuring they don't feel judged or diminished.

Watching someone cry can be tough, especially because it can make us feel emotional too. We might feel empathy and want to comfort them, but at the same time, we could feel unsure about how to help in that moment. It's a mix of wanting to support them but also feeling a bit lost. Not knowing what to do can make the situation feel more awkward for both you and the other person.

So, what to do if somebody cries in front of you?

Strategy 1: Let it happen

Let them cry. Let them be. Be quiet and give this person room. Crying is just a form of communication and sometimes we need to cry to make ourselves known, to release our body from stress or to just get it out of our system. It's a temporary release, typically lasting a few minutes but if we try to repress it, things might get worse. If you can show to the crying person that it's okay that they cry, that you don't stress because of it yourself and that you see it as a normal behaviour, then it will be okay.

Strategy 2: Offer help

Some individuals may apologize while crying, but you can reassure them by saying, 'It's okay. You're allowed to cry and I'm here for you if you need to talk.' You can offer your support by asking if there's anything you can do for them. They might decide to open up about their situation or they may need some time before responding. Either way it's important to offer support in a way that aligns with their needs. They may even ask for some space, like requesting that you leave the room for a while, and respecting that boundary is another way to offer help.

The downfall with asking questions is the fact that it triggers a switch into thinking mode. It can push their feelings to the side because they feel obligated to answer you. Instead, sometimes it's more helpful to simply be present and let them know, 'Whatever you need, I'm here for you.' This approach offers support without demanding an immediate shift from feeling to explaining.

Strategy 3: Offer a pacifying object

You might want to offer a tissue, a glass of water or a shoulder to cry on, but it's important not to do it out of obligation. Make sure you don't do this as a mechanical gesture. I clearly remember the first time I took my driver's exam and didn't pass. When the examiner told me I had failed, his tone was so flat and mechanical that it felt like he was reading from a script. As if on autopilot, while he was delivering the message he pulled out a box of tissues from his desk drawer. It was such a strange, rehearsed move that I couldn't help but laugh out loud. I wasn't crying like he was expecting; in fact, I was doing the opposite – I laughed because of the awkwardness of the situation.

The idea of offering something is perfect but don't do it if you don't mean it.

Strategy 4: Create a lighter atmosphere

Adding a bit of lightness to the situation can help ease any tension. Whether it's an appropriate joke or casually acknowledging the awkwardness of the moment, people often appreciate it. Just be mindful of the context and the people involved. When done right, a little humour can really help lighten the mood. Once I was sobbing with snot running down my nose. Observing me, my manager at the time said, 'Seems like you're in real need of a tissue.' He said it in such a way that we both cracked up laughing. It wasn't mean or inappropriate; he knew how to lighten the mood without ignoring what was actually going on.

Strategy 5: Use your body language

When you use your body language effectively, you can make a big difference in how you connect with others. For instance, leaning in slightly shows that you're engaged and actively listening, signalling to the other person that you care about what they're saying. You can give others space by adjusting your posture, or stepping back can make them feel more at ease and less pressured. Tilting your head is another powerful gesture; it demonstrates that you're listening and that you're not a threat, which can help someone feel more comfortable and understood. By being aware of your body language, you create an open and inviting atmosphere that encourages more meaningful interactions.

Strategy 6: Focus on the content, not the emotion

Tears can be distracting, but don't let them throw you off. Stay focused on your message and continue repeating what you want to say until it's understood. Be patient, as it may take time for the other person to be receptive to listening. If emotions become overwhelming, consider rescheduling the conversation to ensure effective communication.

I once assisted a manager who was dealing with a highly emotional colleague. This individual would start crying at the slightest misunderstanding or feedback. It often felt disproportionate to the situation, creating an emotional situation that made open dialogue difficult. The manager genuinely wanted to help but felt unsure of what to do, as the tears made him hesitant to say anything at all.

When it comes to someone crying, know what is important to you and what you are comfortable with in various situations. Clearly express your boundaries to others in a respectful and direct manner if needed.

If the emotional response feels overwhelming, not genuine or out of proportion to the situation, it's okay to step in and set some boundaries. Use 'I' statements to convey your needs and feelings without blaming or criticizing: 'I really want to listen to you to find out what is going on but if you are crying there is no conversation possible.' This helps others understand your limits and reduces confusion: 'I truly want to give you space to express how you're feeling and I can see this is important to you. At the same time, we need to keep our focus on the project, so let's look at what we can do to move things forward and, if needed, we can talk more about the emotional side in a separate moment.'

Strategy 7: Don't do it alone

If you sense that emotions will be a big part of the conversation and especially if you expect someone might be crying frequently, it can be a good idea to bring someone from HR along to provide support and guidance. If all goes well, HR staff are trained to manage difficult conversations, maintain confidentiality and ensure everything is handled according to company policies.

Having them there can make the discussion feel more neutral and professional, which can lead to better communication and problem-solving. Plus, they can help with any legal or policy questions that come up. It's a way to make sure the conversation goes smoothly and everyone feels respected.

Conclusion

It's important to note that people cry for various reasons, and it is a normal and healthy emotional response. Crying can help us process emotions, strengthen social bonds and promote overall well-being. It is an essential part of the human experience and a way for us to express and understand our emotions. When someone cries in front of you, be ready to adjust your behaviour to support them if necessary. It's important to be professional in a working setting and remember that crying is a natural part of being human. And when it comes to behaviour that crosses the line, it's important to set boundaries and focus on the content rather than the tears.

CHAPTER THIRTY

What to do if someone is angry and I need to de-escalate a situation?

When people are angry with you or with each other and maybe even start shouting, you might feel like running away and not getting involved at all. But that's not always an option and it's not always the best idea either. As a professional you need to be able to listen to people when they are irritated and angry. Failing to take action in the presence of conflict can escalate the situation. It's essential to possess the skills to de-escalate a situation, even when you're not directly involved. For managers, in particular, not intervening can have severe consequences for the team. If you are not helping the situation, you are not setting an example and you are not creating a trustworthy environment.

There is a short video available online of a police officer skilfully handling a man threatening him with a knife. Surprisingly, all that is needed to defuse the situation is a heartfelt conversation from the sitting officer and the video ends with a comforting hug. We can learn from this video by not being afraid of tense situations and understanding that our behaviour can influence others to become calmer and kinder.

I was working as a host/security staff at a lively party, where I saw a young man engaged in a heated argument with two other guests. His aggressive demeanour led to pushing and shouting, escalating tension among everyone involved.

Unlike the others who matched his anger, I took a different approach. I calmly walked up to him and spoke gently. By carefully listening while others were addressing him, I learned his name and, instead of mirroring his agitation, I shifted the dynamic. With a lower and calmer tone, I addressed him directly: 'Vincent, Vincent...' As he caught his name amidst the commotion, I approached with caution. Gently, I placed a hand on his chest and positioned myself between him and the other two men, creating a physical barrier. With a calm demeanour, I addressed him directly: 'Vincent, what is it you NEED right now?'

He shifted his focus to me, his words tumbling out as he tried to articulate the source of his anger. Patiently, I interrupted him: 'But Vincent, what do you NEED right now? How can we help you at this moment?' My tone was gentle and warm.

Suddenly, he turned to me and began to soften. 'It's okay... It's just that...' he said, his tone calming as he began to tell his story once more. 'Yes, I see. That's really not pleasant at all', and I added, 'I'm truly sorry to hear that', despite the fact that I couldn't fully make sense of what he was trying to explain. I calmed my breathing, and I asked him, 'Are you going to be alright now? Can you return to enjoying the evening with your friends, because you are here to have fun, right?' He looked at his companions, who seemed equally taken aback by the shift. Encouragingly, I said, 'Come on, Vincent, I hope you have a fantastic time. Go and have fun with your friends again.' 'Yes, we will have fun!' he agreed, letting out a cathartic exhale and his expression brightening remarkably. Gratefully, he hugged me, saying 'thank you' before heading back to his group.

A similar thing happened when I encountered a distressing situation where two adult men were engaged in a heated argument, even with one man's young daughter present. Seeing that scene was a little bit scary, and I hesitated to step in because of the fear they would attack me. But I had to do something. Most people make things worse by yelling so I knew I had to do something else.

What proved helpful in this particular case was my approach. I approached the men from an angle, lowered my voice and gently touched their arms to get their attention. I calmly addressed them, saying, 'Guys, dear guys... what's happening here? There is a child present, listening to you both, and I think I can assume this is not the way you want to talk in front of a small, frightened kid, right?' I used my open hand to point out where the girl was listening and they could see the fear in her eyes.

By maintaining a calm attitude and emphasizing the presence of the child, I aimed to defuse the situation and draw attention to the inappropriateness of their behaviour.

I spoke slowly, calmly and with empathy. To my surprise, they paused, still showing signs of anger, but glanced at the child. I stepped between them, gently guiding one away, saying, 'It's okay, she's alright.' Though they kept mumbling, one eventually walked off. The man with the child looked a bit embarrassed. After quickly checking on the girl, I asked if anyone needed a drink to ease the tension.

All the things I did can help you as well when you want to de-escalate a conversation. Let's examine a few of them.

Strategy 1: Stay calm and prioritize emotional harmony

If you choose to intervene in a situation, you must be prepared and skilled enough not to escalate it further. Our priority is the safety of everyone involved. If you decide to step in, maintain your calm and focus, even when emotions run high. You have to keep your ego in check and prioritize emotional harmony over being right. You might want to address what's going on but make sure you are not verbally or nonverbally attacking them. The goal is to de-escalate, not to criticize or blame the person showing the emotion. It's about addressing an emotional issue with the aim of achieving emotional balance. This means putting our own feelings aside and focusing on a resolution, using our skills to create emotional harmony.

Take deep breaths and try to remain centred and calm, even in emotionally charged situations. The emotion you take into the setting will influence the people you are trying to calm down.

Strategy 2: Use your voice

Communicate with a calm and lowered tone of voice. We like that calming voice that our parents or educators use to soothe us when we are children. Have you ever listened to people singing lullabies; they are kind and soothing and we use a low tone. Using that same key to address others in a distressing situation will evoke a calmer reaction than a high, screechy and shooting voice.

Consciously slow down your speech, speak slower than you normally would and relax your vocal cords. Also, focus on breathing deeply and evenly to maintain a steady and soothing tone. Chris Voss, in his book *Never Split the Difference* (2016) accurately calls this the DJ voice.

Additionally, it's not just lowering your voice in a calm and soothing way, it's also WHAT you say.

Strategy 3: Use words and positive language

Use your words to create a more positive atmosphere. Saying someone's name grabs their attention and also makes the interaction more personal. You can guide them with specific words to create a shift in their mindset. It will lead them in more positive directions, moving from anger to enjoyment, as shown in the example above. This technique can redirect the conversation towards themes like friendship, 'fun' and good times. In a business context, using terms such as 'teamwork', 'collaboration', 'getting along' and 'safety' can similarly guide discussions towards more constructive and harmonious outcomes. It's all about steering the conversation in a friendly and more constructive direction. When individuals are exposed to positive words and expressions, they tend to become more motivated to engage, listen actively and work collaboratively in problem-solving situations. Talk about what is possible instead of what isn't possible. For instance, instead of saying, 'I know this task is impossible' you can say, 'Let's find a way to make this work'.

Strategy 4: Ask questions and listen

You can ask open-ended questions to encourage the other person to express their experiences and perspectives. For instance, if you're trying to understand a situation better, you might ask, 'What has happened?' This allows the person to provide more detail, helping you grasp the context. This way, they can give you all the details you need to understand the situation better. But the real reason is, you're also letting them vent and release all that built-up negative energy. If someone's really ticked off, let them blow off steam by ranting, yelling and shouting. Eventually, they'll wear themselves out and calm down, much like a balloon slowly deflating as the air is let out. It's a natural way for pent-up emotions to release.

For example, asking, 'What do you need right now?' made Vincent pause and reflect. It steered him away from his bad experiences and let him focus on the now. Asking what was needed in the moment helped Vincent to snap out of the past. When you ask a question, carefully listen to their message and acknowledge what they are saying.

Strategy 5: Show genuine interest and empathy

Acknowledging and validating what a person is saying or what they have gone through is very important in de-escalation. People want to feel seen and heard, and genuine acknowledgement can make a big difference. In customer service, we often hear scripted, insincere lines like 'I'm sorry, sir, I can't help' or 'I'm sorry, that's not in my job description'. This kind of response can feel fake and unhelpful. In contrast, a sincere expression of empathy can work wonders. For example, saying, 'I'm truly sorry for what has happened to you' or 'I'm sorry that you had to experience this' with the right tone can convey genuine concern and understanding. This approach not only helps to de-escalate the situation but also builds trust and rapport with the person.

Show genuine interest in the other person; what are they feeling and what are their experiences? By asking thoughtful questions and giving them time to reflect, you'll be surprised how often they realize on their own that they don't want to shout or remain angry. You don't have to agree with the content but by showing genuine interest and empathy towards the other person's feelings and experiences, you will calm the situation. You might say something like, 'It sounds like you're really frustrated and I can understand why that might be upsetting'. By reflecting back their feelings, you show them you see and hear them, which helps them feel validated.

Strategy 6: Use your body language

It's crucial to be mindful of our body language, especially in tense situations. Using our body in these moments can really make a difference. We want to show comfort through our body movements to influence others. So, keep your shoulders relaxed, stand with an open posture and avoid crossing your arms or legs. Use simple gestures like arching your eyebrows, head tilting, nodding or smiling if appropriate. Genuinely show you're listening and create a positive but also serious atmosphere. Also, your tone and tempo of voice is important. Remember the DJ voice?

Maintain a respectful physical distance, especially when someone is angry. Give them space and avoid getting too close or invading their personal area. Prioritize your safety and carefully assess the situation before approaching.

Even though I stepped in to create a barrier between agitated people, it wasn't to escalate things but to calm them down. I knew it was the right move because I observed the situation closely and I understand the nuances in human behaviours. By creating a physical but non-threatening barrier between two people I aimed to shift the focus and energy of the confrontation. My approach was quick and effective, aiming to introduce a pause in the escalation and offer escape for all to create a new setting. But also avoid getting too close to the other person or invading their personal space or belongings. Never forget that context is key. What works in one situation may not be appropriate in another, so it's crucial to adjust your behaviour accordingly.

Strategy 7: Change the scenery

Think about changing up the surroundings, such as going for a walk or sitting together, to help relax the atmosphere. If things start to get more intense, taking a break could be a good idea to let everyone cool down. For example, in an office setting, you might suggest stepping out into the hallway or outside to ease the tension. Walking to the coffee machine to get a drink might have the same effect.

While working with a very tense team, I decided to take them out of the conference room to help everyone cool off. I asked each person to speak privately with the colleague they felt had a problem or misunderstanding during the meeting. Taking these conversations outside, away from the pressure of the conference room, really helped to improve the atmosphere and ease tensions.

You can relieve tension by going for a walk or sitting side by side. Sometimes it helps to take one of the people involved in the argument out of the room for a quick chat. For example, you might say, 'Hey Mark, let's grab a cup of coffee before we continue the conversation.'

Leaving the situation allows everyone to regroup, calm down and reflect on what's really happening. Consider taking a break to give everyone a chance to cool off. This could be just a few minutes, or, in some cases, returning to the issue the next day might be more beneficial. For example, you could say, 'How about we meet tomorrow to discuss this further before we proceed?'

Conclusion

De-escalation techniques are invaluable. Having the ability to de-escalate confrontations can prevent conflict, prevent harm from happening and can even reduce the risk of violence and ensure a more positive experience for all parties involved. By learning these strategies, you can create a safer and more effective environment. When you know how to calm tensions, you're not just improving outcomes – you're building stronger, more respectful relationships with colleagues and clients.

Remember, every situation is different, so it's important to adjust these tips to fit your specific circumstances. Don't hesitate to ask what's needed; people may be open to sharing how you can help de-escalate. But keep in mind, doing nothing is the least helpful option. Take action and you'll see better outcomes!

CHAPTER THIRTY-ONE

What to do if I don't want to hire toxic people?

A great company begins with hiring the right people.

While many companies review CVs, conduct interviews and assess skills, you'd be surprised at how many don't. Many also neglect to check references and backgrounds. Do we really know the names listed as references and do we take the time to contact them for verification? We ask questions during job interviews, but do we actually observe the answers? Do we even meet with the interviewee to observe their nonverbal communication? Do we take people at their word without digging deeper?

We must be mindful of the significant impact people can have on our colleagues, our clients and our company. Some may seem friendly and adequate in the moment, but it's important to ask ourselves: is this genuine? Or is it simply an act to make a good impression and secure the job? It's crucial to pick up on subtle signals early, as hiring the wrong person means giving them influence over your team and possibly even sensitive company information. It's about recognizing whether their behaviour is authentic or if they are simply showing their best side to get hired. If you bring certain individuals on board, it could mean that you give the power to influence others in a way that might not align with your company's values. Their actions, attitudes and behaviours can shape the work environment, affecting relationships, decision-making and overall morale. They could create an uncomfortable or toxic environment, so we must be extra thorough.

There are many stories about toxic personalities and the chaos they leave behind after being fired (if you're lucky enough to be able to fire them). Typically, there are two types of reactions from the company afterwards: either 'We didn't notice it at all' or 'Everyone knew, but no one dared to speak up'.

When a manager finally gets fired after yet another aggressive outburst, people often say, 'Finally, they took action. This person has been terrorizing the team for years.' It makes you wonder how disruptive personalities even get hired in the first place and, even more puzzling, how they manage to stick around for so long. It's always intriguing to me how it is possible for people to create so much damage before any action is taken.

It's essential to ensure that the person you hire will contribute positively to the team dynamic and respond appropriately in various situations. So, what to do?

Strategy 1: Check! Check! Double check!

As part of your due diligence process, you should thoroughly check and verify information.

Always read the CV carefully. Some people skim through it or overlook details that stand out. I once heard about a case where someone didn't notice that a candidate had changed jobs almost every year. On the surface, it seemed like they had a lot of experience, but the timeline revealed a pattern. It turned out that the person had trouble keeping a job due to their personality, which caused issues in the workplace. If you pay attention to these details, you might gain valuable insights into a candidate's true fit for the role.

Check their LinkedIn profile for inconsistencies with the resume. Lack of professional recommendations or an empty profile can be potential red flags that warrant further investigation. You can also check other platforms like Facebook or Instagram to also check the cultural fit: it can give you clues about a candidate's interests and values, which can help determine if they are a good cultural fit for the company.

Check references thoroughly, and don't just stop at their boss. Talk to former colleagues to learn more about the candidate's teamwork skills, how they get along with others and how they handle everyday situations at work. By reaching out to both supervisors and colleagues, you'll get a more honest and complete picture of the candidate's strengths, weaknesses and overall job performance.

Ask for a copy of diplomas and degrees: sometimes it's helpful to request both physical and digital copies of all relevant qualifications. While this might seem a bit overcautious, some employers have discovered discrepancies in candidates' backgrounds that weren't initially obvious. Though many Hollywood movies have been made around this premise, in reality, hiring someone with false qualifications can be disastrous for a business.

Sometimes, if something feels too good to be true, it might actually be. For example, a woman with an impressive resume was later found out to be pretending. She claimed to have graduated from multiple programmes, but in reality, she had only completed one. The HR manager had a gut feeling something wasn't right, as he had never seen a resume that outstanding in his entire career. The suspicions were eventually confirmed.

Strategy 2: Observe before the interview

One of the things that stands out is what candidates do before the actual interview. How do they present themselves online? How do they interact in emails, over the phone or with staff? For example, there was a candidate who, before their interview, posted on social media, 'I'm going to get that job, no doubt. Time to make some serious money!' This post came across as arrogant, rude and solely focused on the financial aspect of the role, rather than showing genuine interest in the company or the work itself. This kind of attitude raised concerns about their professionalism and overall fit for the team.

Another thing to observe is how candidates treat staff. I once saw a lady completely ignore a staff member who kindly brought her a coffee before the interview. Now, it could have been nerves, but those are the small moments that stand out to me and make me start to wonder. How someone treats others – especially when they don't think they're being watched – can reveal a lot about their true character.

Strategy 3: Make feelings count

Sometimes it's all perfect on paper and the job interview is perfect but something is off.

I once worked with a woman who had a hard time explaining why she didn't feel comfortable being alone in a room with a particular colleague. She had a gut feeling about him from the start, even during the interview, but he performed well and was hired. He had never done anything directly to her, but something about him just didn't sit right. Later, it came to light that he had a history of being very pushy towards women and had crossed boundaries in his previous job by hugging a woman against her will. Some might call it intuition, but it's actually the neurons in our stomach that warn us about certain behaviours. Our survival instincts have already picked up on the subtle signals. *The Gift of Fear* by Gavin de Becker (2000) is a fascinating book that explores this phenomenon, showing how our bodies can sense danger before our minds fully process it.

Strategy 4: Decide with the team

One piece of advice is to create a committee with individuals from different divisions, backgrounds and cultures. Each of us brings a unique perspective shaped by our experiences, so while we may notice different things, we might also observe the same behaviours. However, those behaviours might affect us in different ways, depending on our individual roles, backgrounds and cultural influences. This diversity in viewpoints can lead to more well-rounded observations and better decision-making.

Sometimes it's a good idea to involve the whole team in the decision-making process. In small companies or close teams, it's important that everyone has a say. Rather than solely relying on the team leader or manager to decide on new hires, working with a collaborative decision-making process could be beneficial. This could be done anonymously or by voting democratically, where the majority rules.

If you involve everyone it can help build stronger connections within the team and get everyone on board with the new hire. It also brings in different perspectives, which leads to more balanced decisions. For example, if 80 per cent of the team says yes, you might lean towards a 'yes' for bringing that candidate on board. But it's also important to pay attention to any concerns or objections, as this method could point out potential issues early. Sometimes an observant colleague might notice something others missed, and those concerns are definitely worth considering before making a final decision.

Strategy 5: Create an assessment

'Actions speak louder than words' is a great saying to understand the importance of behaviour. It's something we should all remember as professionals. During a job interview, assessments can help you observe someone's behaviour in specific situations. Even though the setting is created, seeing someone handle pressure in real life is far more revealing than just hearing them say they can. Watching their reactions lets you spot strengths and potential challenges much more clearly than talking about them alone. A good assessment also provides the candidate with tips on their performance, giving you another opportunity to see how they handle criticism and interact in response.

Strategy 6: Ask for examples

When we do our diligence we check with former management, but not a lot of people to talk to former co-workers. Working with someone gives a different perspective than managing them and knowing about their day-to-day interactions can offer great insights into their behaviour on the job.

Try asking about their pitfalls to see if they have genuine self-reflection. When doing so it's important to ask for specific examples. How do they work in a team? What do they do if someone doesn't listen? Can they share a mistake they made when dealing with others? Analyse if they can identify their behaviour and the effect it has on others. Look for signs like a constant need for admiration, lack of empathy, manipulation and a sense of entitlement.

Asking a narcissist if they're a narcissist probably won't get you an honest answer. They usually lack self-awareness and might not recognize or admit to their traits. It's generally better to observe how they act and interact.

You might be surprised, though. I once had a person give some examples of past situations and after listening, I said, 'To be honest, the way you describe yourself and the situations you've been in sounds a bit narcissistic. In your story, you seem to blame others without reflecting on your own behaviour. Would you consider yourself a bit narcissistic?' He replied, 'Yeah, I guess you could say I am. I just want things done my way. If people can't handle it, they can leave. Honestly, most people are too stupid to understand how things should be done. They just need to listen to me and do what I say.'

Strategy 7: Inform yourself about toxic people's behaviour

I often give talks on toxic behaviour and how to handle it. It's surprising how many HR managers and other leaders are caught off guard by specific toxic behaviours. These behaviours can be mislabelled or go unnoticed, and sometimes, even when HR notices them, they are overruled by management, making it challenging to address the problem effectively from the start.

HR professionals and management teams are usually good with general policies but may miss subtle toxic signs like passive-aggressive comments or undermining colleagues. These actions can be mistaken for strong leadership or high standards, preventing real issues from being addressed.

Toxic behaviours are sometimes overlooked or brushed off as simple personality conflicts, rather than being recognized as harmful patterns of behaviour. This can lead to a workplace culture that tolerates these negative behaviours. The point is that it's important to identify and address these behaviours right from the hiring process, so they don't make their way into the workplace and affect the team.

An HR manager once warned against hiring a particular candidate because of his negative behaviour towards her staff, but the board decided to hire him anyway. Unfortunately, he later caused significant issues with his bullying behaviour and his contract was ultimately not renewed. Had the board listened to the HR manager's advice, much of the damage could have been prevented.

In my talks, I emphasize the need for everyone in leadership to be proactive in identifying and addressing toxic behaviours. I provide practical tools like anonymous reporting systems, regular team feedback sessions and training in verbal and nonverbal behaviour and conflict resolution. But honestly, the best approach is to start right from the hiring process so you can keep toxic people out of your organization from the get-go.

Conclusion

Raising awareness is key to creating healthier workplaces. By educating HR managers, CEOs and other leaders and giving them the tools to spot and handle toxic behaviours from the very start of the hiring process, we can help build a more positive and productive work environment. It's not just about stopping negative behaviour; it's about creating a space where people feel safe, respected and valued – something that benefits everyone in the long run.

Stay alert and trust your instincts. If something feels off about a candidate, don't hesitate to say no, even if you can't pinpoint exactly why. Your gut feeling is picking up on things you might not even be aware of, and it's valuable information. That uncomfortable feeling could be a sign of something deeper, and it's better to listen to it than risk bringing in someone who could cause trouble down the road.

CHAPTER THIRTY-TWO

What to do if I work with someone who has narcissistic traits?

Do you work with a toxic individual? We're not psychologists, so it's not our role to label people and we should be cautious about doing so. But we can, and should, observe behaviour carefully. We learn about people by observing their behaviour, which helps us understand their tendencies and preferences. This understanding guides us in adapting our interactions for better outcomes. However, when we are dealing with toxic individuals, it requires a whole new level of attention and consideration.

When we notice behaviour affecting us negatively, it's time to take action. If the impact is so strong that it leaves us feeling really uncomfortable or even physically unwell, it becomes crucial to figure out what we can do to handle the situation. We need to make sure we set clear boundaries and create a healthy work environment to empower ourselves. But before getting into strategies, let's assess if we're dealing with someone who has narcissistic traits.

If you want to be thorough in your analysis, former FBI agent Joe Navarro and I created a very helpful and extensive list with observations for work settings. The BAI© (Behavioural Assessment Inventory) is a practical assessment tool specifically designed for business managers, executives, corporate security and HR personnel to identify problematic individuals. The tool is based on Joe Navarro's compelling book *Dangerous Personalities* (2014), which I highly recommend. The book gives very useful insights into multiple traits from people flawed of character, and he has generously allowed us to use some of his material. For this short chapter I will use a practical approach and highlight a few important traits you might experience in your workplace.

People with narcissistic traits have a grandiose idea of who they are; they overvalue themselves and their capabilities, and devalue others as being inferior, incapable or not worthy. They are exploitative of others and take advantage of others for personal gain. They act like bullies, have a need to control others and demand loyalty at all times. They compete with peers for attention or praise. They fail to view things from another perspective and lack empathy. They are unwilling to acknowledge mistakes and wrongdoings, will lie and have no self-reflection. They are excessively self-centred and are arrogant in their behaviour. They will not let go of grievances and will torment others.

What stands out is their oppressive behaviour within social interactions. In other words, they try to put you down. Working with these individuals is not only soul-crushing, it's stomach-turning. When encountering these toxic individuals, we need a proactive strategy for how to deal with them. If you don't take action, you'll face it nearly every day because of the persistence of the behaviour. It will happen again and again until the effect it has on you could literally make you sick.

We have to realize that if we don't take care of it ourselves the situation won't change. We will be belittled, yelled at, ignored.

They will take credit for our work, they won't care about our well-being, they will be rigid and harsh in their demands and will show scorn if we don't play by their rules.

If we notice two or three of these traits, there's no cause for concern, as we all possess some narcissistic traits. However, if you observe an abundance of these traits, this is the individual being discussed in this chapter. If you come across this person in your day-to-day work it's helpful to apply the strategies below to help yourself and others.

Strategy 1: Know your limits

Consider how long you can endure such behaviour. Whether it's a short internship, a year until retirement or an indefinite period, ask yourself: is this sustainable? While finding new jobs might not be easy, sometimes a lower paygrade could be better than enduring daily mistreatment. Know that the best way to deal with these individuals is to distance yourself from them. If you choose to stay, make the most of it, stand your ground and be prepared to explore other options. If you find yourself in this situation, try to find ways to navigate through it while prioritizing your well-being and seeking potential opportunities for improvement.

Strategy 2: Keep a journal/notebook/diary

It's wise to register the correspondence and conversations you have with the narcissist. The most heard comment when working with people with narcissistic traits is that they will try to dodge a bullet by denying and twisting everything you say about them. They will say you misinterpret them. They might say you are making things up or that what you are claiming they said is not true. Everything that you have on record with dates, times and describing specific observed behaviour will help you in future situations where you might have to tell HR or others what has happened. Email yourself about the day you had, take notes. I have sometimes encouraged people to openly record meetings to ensure there is no room for evading accountability. Even though the person knows about the implemented measure, they can still attempt to distort facts and shift blame onto others, but this time, there is no denying their actions.

Strategy 3: Set boundaries

People like Gandhi and Nelson Mandela have taught us that dignity is inside of you. As Alice Walker said: 'The most common way people give up their power is by thinking they don't have any.'

So many things have been said to put people down and they can come in all forms. It could be blunt and aggressive, like 'Fetch me some coffee, now!' or 'You're too young to speak in this meeting, you're nothing', or even 'So well done... for a woman.' But it can also be more subtle, like 'Oh, that's a good idea, for someone with your experience' or 'You're doing well for someone who's still new around here.' At first glance, these comments might seem complimentary, but they're actually designed to undermine someone's confidence and minimize their achievements. Whether overt or subtle, these remarks are intended to make others feel smaller or less capable. They belittle your achievements, trying to diminish your potential.

First and foremost, recognize that such statements are not acceptable. Don't hesitate to pause the meeting and stand up for yourself.

Don't be afraid to repeat yourself, ask questions and summarize key points to make sure your contributions are heard and acknowledged.

This could even lead to the decision to leave your job, but if that's not an option, vocalize your boundaries clearly. For instance, you can say, 'This is belittling and I don't appreciate the way you are speaking to me.' Claim your right to be treated with respect.

Strategy 4: Find others to help you

A toxic person, like a narcissist, will often try to devalue you in front of a group. However, they don't always display this behaviour in a public setting; sometimes they choose quieter, more subtle moments, targeting individuals when no one else is around. And you might not be the only one who experiences this behaviour. When a group unites against the toxic individual, it becomes harder for them to continue their bullying behaviour. Group pressure can be a powerful tool in stopping this behaviour, as it challenges their attempts to manipulate or belittle others.

In guided team sessions I often train people to vent what they experience working together. When they start to speak up and realize they have similar experiences with a certain toxic person, strategies can be combined. By joining forces, they can shift the power dynamics. In different cases the toxic boss had to come to their senses.

For some people it might seem far-fetched to make an official complaint. People hesitate because they don't want to be seen as 'difficult'. However, it's advisable to schedule a meeting or at least email others about your encounters with the toxic individual. HR will be grateful if they gain knowledge about what is going on. Warning your manager about your toxic colleague could be a wise idea. Your manager might not see what happens in day-to-day work settings, so informing them is key. Only then can they act and change the situation.

Strategy 5: Change your language

Using phrases like 'maybe', 'I'm not sure' or 'sorry' can weaken your assertiveness and firmness. When you constantly use these sentences, you may unintentionally undermine your credibility and weaken your position in conversations. Such language makes you appear indecisive or lacking in confidence. Instead, opt for direct statements and shorter sentences like 'I don't want to do this' or 'This is a no for me'. By using more definitive language, you will improve your ability to set clear and strong boundaries.

Strategy 6: Find your style of communicating

Some people like to use humour. Once a toxic manager told his peer that he was so proud of her for finding the toilet while visiting a new client's office. This was meant as a belittling moment; she was spoken to like a child. Instead of getting angry or upset, she laughed and said, 'Yes. That surprised me as well. I think I'm way smarter than we might all think I am. I might even need a raise because of this.' He appreciated her joke and the small smile that he showed just said enough.

If you are afraid of talking directly to an individual with narcissistic traits, find a different way. You could ask a colleague to handle the interaction or try communicating through email for some distance. Using the phone or texting can also create a helpful buffer, as it prevents direct confrontation. While you might still hear the narcissist's voice, at least you won't be subjected to direct shouting or confrontation in near proximity.

Strategy 7: Find ways to influence the toxic person

Yes. It can be done. Influencing people with narcissistic traits is possible. Understanding that they love compliments can be valuable knowledge in a workplace. Appeal to their ego: narcissists have a strong desire for admiration and recognition. Compliment their strengths and achievements to gain favour and cooperation.

In meetings this becomes particularly challenging when the chairperson is a toxic individual. Instead of turn-yielding it often becomes a power struggle to determine who will have the 'honour' of speaking. In such situations, it is crucial to assert yourself and get attention through your body language. Raise your arm or actively request an opportunity to speak. In a toxic environment, it becomes essential to take charge and act as your own chairperson.

Additionally, understanding their motivations can allow you to frame your ideas and suggestions in a way that aligns with their desires. For example, if a narcissist values status, emphasize how your proposal can enhance their reputation or position within the company.

Sometimes, playing your part might help you navigate a toxic situation.

Conclusion

Dealing with toxic people in the workplace can be challenging, but there are various strategies to deal with such behaviour effectively. Ultimately, the key takeaway is that maintaining inner strength and dignity is crucial when facing toxic individuals in the workplace. Whatever you go through, keep your strength and hold your head up high and seek help. You are not alone!

As Joe Navarro wisely advises, 'You have no obligation to let yourself be victimized. EVER!'

CHAPTER THIRTY-THREE

What to do if I work with a colleague with paranoid traits?

'Where have you been, what are you doing?'
'What is happening with that project? Why was I not informed?'
'What were you guys talking about?'
'What are you writing down?'
'You went to lunch without me, didn't you? Why?'

Working with a colleague who is showing paranoid behaviour is not only exhausting, it's also uncomfortable and keeps you on edge all the time.

It's not just asking questions. The paranoid personality is someone who is highly suspicious of whatever is happening. They have a disproportionate view on things that happen and are very rigid in their thinking.

When decisions are made within the company, this individual often interprets them as personal attacks. When a rule changes in a company, for instance to change passwords every month for safety, they interpret this as a decision that violates their freedom. 'Why do they do this? It's to influence us all, to keep us on a leash!' Or when they find out they haven't been informed about something (even regarding a project they have nothing to do with), they will make it personal: 'You never tell me anything. You guys are all against me!'

For example, I was informed about a person who filed a complaint after being politely asked to correct a small mistake. They claimed they were 'humiliated' and 'treated like a child' because of the gentle correction. They exaggerated how they had been 'publicly embarrassed' by the situation, suggesting it was likely just an excuse to fire them. This person was overly sensitive to small correction.

Their suspicion extends to various aspects, whether directed at specific individuals, entire teams, opposing groups or even new competitors whom they distrust, including computers or phones. Technology can be dangerous and 'others' even more so.

I once witnessed a group of happy individuals receiving gift cards as a reward for their outstanding performance. The manager had generously allowed them to select a gift of their choice worth €50 from an online store because of their hard work. However, one person reacted differently. They immediately became wary, questioning the motive behind the gift cards, expressing concerns about potential monitoring of their gift choices and viewing it as an intrusion of privacy, likening it to the concept of 'Big Brother is watching you'.

Naturally, his scepticism and anger dampened the spirits of the entire team, who had been genuinely pleased that their efforts were being recognized. For a manager, dealing with such behaviour can feel like a burden. Individuals with a paranoid mindset will scrutinize every action you take and compel you to justify even the smallest decisions. It's important to note that they are likely never to be fully satisfied with any explanation you provide, as their fundamental issue lies with trust.

So, what are our options?

Strategy 1: Be as open as possible

By opening up within the boundaries of the company, you will allow this kind of employee to see what's happening. They often doubt the intentions and actions of others and are suspicious without a cause, so if there is no need to hold something back, don't! I have trained managers who were reluctant to do this because of the feeling that everything you say can and will be used against you. But if it's something that you can already share don't hold back. That way trust starts to grow. Again, you don't share want you can't share but if you know information can be out in the open don't sit on it.

Strategy 2: Be clear regarding your actions

I coached a manager who was dealing with a person with paranoid traits. They are highly judgmental and seek control and impose strict rules and expectations. I emphasized the importance of clear, precise communication. Vague assurances like 'I will look into that' tend to be ineffective. Instead, clear communication can make a significant difference. For instance, saying, 'I will look into that and provide you with an update next Monday during our meeting at 10' can offer a sense of predictability and structure, which helps to ease out concerns and create a calmer environment.

Strategy 3: Be clear regarding your limits

Another manager was constantly on edge because one highly judgmental employee kept coming to him, day in and day out, with all sorts of things she'd picked up around the office – whispers she caught, scenarios she figured he was unaware of. She not just dumped information; she always had a list of directives ready for him to go with it: cancel that project, fire this person, deny that vacation request. It was a lot.

Also, this person filed a complaint against a coworker. They were working together, and she described the cooperation as 'completely unprofessional' and 'a clear sign of disrespect'.

The manager took the grievance very seriously and conducted a thorough investigation to ensure that all aspects of the situation were carefully reviewed. After looking into the matter in detail, it became clear that the employee had highly exaggerated the events. It turned out that a certain email wasn't responded to within an hour.

The manager was pretty unsure how to handle it, but together, we got him to a place where he could respond with firm, straightforward replies:

> I'm sorry you felt disrespected and I took your concerns seriously, which is why I conducted a thorough investigation. However, certain elements of the situation seem to have been overstated with an emotional reaction that appeared disproportionate to the events themselves. While I value your feedback, it's important we focus on the facts and address real concerns constructively. I know how you value honesty so let's work together to prevent misunderstandings and maintain a positive, respectful environment.

Strategy 4: Set boundaries

While it can be useful to have someone keeping you in the loop as a manager, it becomes a problem if it turns into a habit driven by distrust and disruption. If left unchecked, your team might begin to tiptoe around this person, which can negatively impact collaboration. Moreover, by not addressing the issue, you risk losing your team's trust as a manager and you might lay the foundation for a toxic work environment where people gossip and avoid each other. Acting is crucial to maintaining a healthy work environment and ensuring effective teamwork.

A clear 'no' is essential, accompanied by a warm yet firm halt to actions. It's important to be resolute in delivering the message while maintaining a positive relationship. If the person comes again with additional information about observations, make sure you know the boundaries you want to address:

> Thank you for sharing your thoughts, but I'm not going to take that action. Just to clarify, this isn't part of your responsibilities. Please focus on your role and allow me to handle the management decisions. Going forward, please refrain from further involvement in this matter.

It's also possible that the toxic person might try to keep information for themselves, for a variety of reasons. Being highly cautious, one person consistently refused to update their progress on a project in the company system, being convinced others were using the system to monitor or judge them. The manager stepped in and said, 'This isn't optional; providing updates is part of your job and the team can't function without it.'

Strategy 5: Inform others

People with paranoid traits tend to see things in definite terms: you're either on their side or you're not. If you end up on their 'not' list, be prepared for some negative behaviour. They tent to blame others for failures in their life. They might shun you, show dismissive behaviour or gossip about you. This kind of behaviour can drag on forever unless you show them you're on board with their views and ways of doing things. It can feel like the only way to be accepted is to go along, even when it doesn't sit well with you.

But we are not kids in the kindergarten playground anymore and you don't have to play by their rules. If you encounter such behaviour, it's important to let someone know. You could mention it to a colleague, but I strongly recommend informing someone from HR or your manager. This way, if things escalate, you won't be facing the situation alone.

Strategy 6: Use knowledge and facts

Providing fact-based information can really help to address a paranoid individual's concerns. Say they are concerned about the budget in a project; if you pull out the actual numbers or documents, it can be a bit of an eye-opener. It shows them straight up that a lot of what they're worried about is just in their head. People who see things in black and white can really benefit from this approach: 'Here, look at the facts, stop worrying.'

Strategy 7: Support them to seek help

I once helped a woman dealing with a lot of distrust and suspicion. She didn't trust her colleagues, felt left out and was under the impression they gossiped about her daily. She didn't experience this only at work but also in her personal life – she didn't trust her neighbours and had stopped going to the gym because she didn't trust anyone there. I listened to her worries and pointed out how draining it must be for her to experience such emotions all the time. I advised her to see a counsellor and she sought help. She started to realize how her scepticism impacted her life and started working on trusting others more. By readdressing her rigid thinking and seeing the behaviour of others in a more positive way, she started to see positive changes in her personal and work relationships as she let go of her preconceived ideas.

Conclusion

Working with someone who exhibits paranoid traits can be extremely challenging, and, in some cases, it's a sign that such an individual should not be hired in the first place. If you do find yourself in a situation where a person with these traits is already on the team, it's crucial to address the issue head-on. While patience and clear, honest communication can help build trust and resolve issues, it's important to recognize that ignoring the problem isn't an option – it can escalate tensions and cause long-term damage to the team dynamic. If a person frequently files exaggerated or paranoid complaints, it can create a toxic work environment, undermining morale and productivity. Offering support or encouraging them to seek professional help is part of the solution, but the company must take swift action to protect the well-being of the team as a whole.

CHAPTER THIRTY-FOUR

What to do if I work with a colleague who is emotionally unstable?

Sometimes we work with people who make us feel very uneasy. Their behaviour is unpredictable and they display emotions that are extreme or overwhelming, often disproportionate to the situation at hand. This doesn't necessarily mean they are crying (see Chapter 29); it could be any intense emotion that feels out of place or misaligned with the context.

This person may display intense emotions such as anger, lashing out, excessive crying, screaming or giving you hostile looks. They might also give the silent treatment or make sudden, unexpected and baseless decisions. These extreme reactions can make working with them exhausting. If you are dealing with someone emotionally unstable, you will often see poorly regulated behaviour and emotions that don't align with the situation. They tend to overreact in ways that are unpredictable and inappropriate, making interactions difficult to navigate. They are both unable and unwilling to manage their emotions in a given situation, making them unreliable in their responses.

As a coworker or boss, dealing with someone with these intense emotions can feel like riding a rollercoaster. One minute they are up, the next they are down. One minute, they appreciate the work you're doing for them, and the next, they're yelling because they feel you're not meeting their needs. They make sudden choices, suddenly change plans or take actions without considering the consequences. For example, they might suddenly decide to take the project in an entirely different direction, without any prior warning, leaving you needing to quickly adjust. These unpredictable shifts make it difficult to keep up and can create a tense, exhausting work environment.

They also seem to 'fall apart' under stress with some frequency, are very sensitive to what others say and think about them and tend to lash out when criticized or when given feedback.

As a colleague, a team member or even as a manager, you find yourself constantly on edge, trying to avoid saying or doing anything that might upset them. You're always on the lookout, adjusting your behaviour to accommodate their mood. It's exhausting to constantly monitor and adapt to their emotional fluctuations. Their mood changes quickly: one moment they're calm, the next they're angry, upset or irritated, often for no obvious reason.

This happens in businesses more often than you think. I have heard an example where employees would anxiously wait by the door to assess their boss's mood. One individual acted as a lookout, quickly sharing the observed mood with others. While we often see such characters in movies and TV shows, working with these kinds of people in real life is a whole different story. It can be draining and stressful.

I witnessed another example during a team meeting. A woman received feedback she perceived as an assault on her hard work. Fuelled by frustration, she seized a mug and threw it with such force that it shattered upon impact with the table. With an explosive outburst, she declared, 'How dare you criticize me!'

A common misconception, however, is that emotionally unstable behaviour is seen only in women. That is not true. We can also see men showing this behaviour, although it might be expressed in a different form because of testosterone. In men, it can show up as a mix of intense anger, antisocial behaviour, substance use and a tendency to seek out new experiences. Although we also see this in women, and it can lead to erratic choices such as ignoring protocols, procedures and social norms.

During a client discussion, a project team member displayed visible signs of disapproval towards the client's comments. This behaviour, including eye-rolling, smirking and tutting, occurred while the client was speaking, disrupting the conversation and shocking the client. Such behaviour was highly inappropriate for the situation and the client was not amused.

So, what to do when you work with someone who doesn't show self-awareness or restraint in emotion?

Strategy 1: Ask yourself if it is sustainable

When we're dealing with people who have flaws or exhibit challenging behaviour, it's important to pause and ask ourselves how long we can realistically tolerate their behaviour. More importantly, how long we do want to put up with it? It's not just about enduring the behaviour, but about considering the long-term impact it has on us. We need to reflect on how their behaviour affects our work, our emotional well-being and our overall happiness. If we find that their behaviour is consistently draining, disruptive or harmful, it's crucial to recognize the toll it's taking on us. Once we fully assess the situation, we can make a more informed decision on how to move forward – whether that means setting boundaries, having a difficult conversation or even distancing ourselves. The key is to take care of ourselves, ensuring that we prioritize our mental and emotional health in the process, while also being honest about what we're willing to tolerate in any relationship or work environment.

Strategy 2: Identify your personal limits and needs

Take some time to reflect on what truly matters to you and what you're comfortable with in different situations. You may find that you can tolerate more – or less – than your colleagues, and that's perfectly fine. Just because someone else is okay with being yelled at doesn't mean you have to accept it. Everyone has their own boundaries, and yours might be different. It's important to prioritize your well-being by looking after yourself physically, mentally and emotionally. Setting boundaries is a form of self-care that helps protect your health and happiness. Sometimes, taking a day off can work wonders and provide the reset you need to continue working on the project with this person for another month.

Strategy 3: Communicate assertively

Clearly express yourself while working with this individual. Make sure you know deadlines and the time you are willing to spend on your job. Express your boundaries in a respectful and direct manner. Use 'I' statements to convey your needs and feelings without blaming or criticizing. For example: 'Thank you for your feedback. However, I don't want to be yelled at because to me that is unprofessional and rude. Please lower your voice' (see Chapter 15 for how to give feedback).

Strategy 4: Be consistent

Once you've established your boundaries, stick to them consistently. Don't yield under pressure. For example, if you agree to work late despite previously stating that you don't want to, an emotionally unstable person may see this as a victory and continue to push your limits. Standing your ground provides clarity and reduces confusion. By consistently enforcing your boundaries, you send a clear message about what is acceptable and what is not, helping to create a more respectful and predictable environment. It also helps maintain your own well-being and prevents resentment from building up over time.

Strategy 5: Know the rules

It's helpful to know companies' policies and rules. What is a manager allowed to ask from you? If they cross a line, you can hold them accountable for their actions based on company policies. Knowing the policies helps in resolving conflicts or disputes effectively and fairly. In one instance, when an employee's phone remained inactive over the weekend, this triggered an explosive reaction from their manager, resulting in a series of furious voicemails. The manager sending 25 messages about a single question is excessive behaviour. It was standard practice in the company for everyone to have weekends off, and the person who was being persistently contacted learned about this rule from HR. Armed with that rule they could put a stop to the behaviour.

Strategy 6: Build alliances

Sometimes we think we have to solve it all by ourselves. But know that you are not alone. You can inform your colleagues or HR about what is happening. But also talking about it with your colleagues might help you to come up with new ideas for how to work with this person. It's not to stimulate a gossip culture but a lot of times I see that when people start sharing their experiences, they feel strengthened on how to approach the situation and together they can think outside of the box on how to tackle the problem.

Strategy 7: Document incidents

It's important to keep a record of what is happening.

You can email yourself or write it down in your agenda or diary. Ensure your notes are specific, detailing concerning behaviour or incidents. Include the place, time and specific behaviour observed. For example: 'When I asked about my raise, she screamed at me, slammed her fist on the table, and said, "You ungrateful brat, make sure you work adequately first to begin with".' This writing helps you put into words what you really mean when someone is crossing personal or professional boundaries.

Be sure to document any follow-up actions or responses, as they may be important for context. Keep a record of any witnesses present during the incident, as their accounts could support your claims. By keeping a detailed log, you'll have a clearer picture of any ongoing patterns of inappropriate behaviour and HR will be grateful for it as well because it's harder to work with claims that look like they are unfounded.

Conclusion

When working with an emotionally unstable colleague, it's important to stay calm and maintain your composure. Clearly define and stick to your personal and professional boundaries. Use direct and clear communication to avoid misunderstandings. You can show empathy and understanding but avoid taking on their emotional burdens and demands. If necessary, make sure to involve HR or a supervisor to help manage the situation. Stay safe and maintain your sanity.

The colleagues described in the last three chapters might be draining in terms of energy and time, and you might even find a combination of the traits in one person, so if you can avoid them, it could be beneficial to do so. However, if you have no other option, ensure you navigate the situation in a way that works for you.

CHAPTER THIRTY-FIVE

What to do if I want to communicate nonverbally in a difficult conversation?

As discussed in the chapter about nonverbal cues, they are very important and it's helpful to know certain behaviours and observe them during conversations. The key to effective nonverbal communication is identifying whether someone is comfortable or uncomfortable. Observing these cues can reveal a lot about your conversational partner's feelings and whether your interaction is on the right track. This goes especially for those difficult conversations.

This chapter takes the focus on nonverbal communication a bit further to explain what you can do to use your body language to make the conversation more effective.

If you notice discomfort during a conversation, it could be a sign that you need to adjust your approach. In challenging conversations, when emotions rise, they can overshadow logical thinking and that's when communication becomes tricky. As professionals, it's our role to steer the conversation towards a more comfortable setting. By using our skills effectively, we can create an environment where people feel more at ease, we can help manage emotions – both ours and others.

Below you will find some examples of nonverbal expressions that you can use in an effective way during those difficult conversations. You can use your body language to create more comfort.

Strategy 1: Proximity

Proximity refers to the physical or spatial distance between people. It's important to understand that it plays a crucial role in creating a level of comfort with each other. If someone is too close for your liking it might enhance discomfort and stress.

Managing proximity can be used for effective communication. For instance, standing very close to someone in a culture that values personal space might be seen as intrusive or aggressive, where in cultures where close physical proximity is the norm, it might be viewed as friendly and engaging.

When someone is stressed, it's important to give them some space. Distance yourself and allow the other person room to vent without feeling crowded or overwhelmed. Being too close to someone in a stressful moment can unintentionally heighten the tension. Our personal space is crucial and when someone stands too near, our brain can interpret it as a potential threat, making the situation more intense. Giving the other person physical space helps them feel more comfortable and can reduce feelings of being cornered or judged.

Strategy 2: The voice

The voice is a powerful tool in communication and it's often overlooked as a helpful form of nonverbal communication. It's not just the words we use; the tone, pitch, volume and pace of our voice can significantly impact the message we're trying to convey.

When someone is stressed or when we are in a difficult conversation, a soothing tone can show empathy and reassurance, while a harsh tone might signal frustration or anger. By modulating our voice to match the emotional tone we want to convey, we can enhance understanding and connection with others.

The voice can also be used to get someone's attention and convey competence. When you need something to be done with a certain urgency it's better to use a strong, clear voice than a hesitant or shaky voice that might undermine your credibility. Pauses, emphasis and changes in intonation can create a better flow in a discussion.

The voice is a very important component of nonverbal communication, contributing to the overall meaning and impact of our messages. By being mindful of how we use our voice, we can enhance the effectiveness of our communication and create a more comfortable and engaging interaction for all parties involved. I once coached a manager who spoke without any volume or emphasis, making him hard to notice. He wanted to become more noticeable, because he needed to set some boundaries in his team. We worked on using his voice more assertively. One day, he spoke loudly to his team and a team member responded, 'Ah, now I know you really mean it when you say it's not possible. I finally understand, thank you for being clearer.'

Strategy 3: Head tilt

A head tilt to the side is usually perceived as a positive sign. There are many memes of cute dogs and cats tilting their head to show interest in their owner. The same behaviour is seen in humans. If we add nodding to that behaviour, it shows that you are a person who is not only interested but also active, involved and engaged in the dialogue. Nodding serves as a nonverbal affirmation, signalling agreement or understanding.

Strategy 4: Eye contact

We must be careful not to draw conclusions too quickly when it comes to eye contact because culture is an essential element in the duration of eye contact. But when someone looks at us combined with a head tilt, for instance, it's completely different than someone looking away all the time. If you keep talking after someone breaks eye contact, your message may not be as effective because they might not be fully focused on listening. While it's okay to briefly break eye contact to give the other person space, be mindful of their cues. On the other hand, maintaining steady eye contact can be important if you want to convey seriousness and confidence. It will ensure you come across as engaged and trustworthy. However, whatever you do, avoid looking at your phone or computer during the conversation. It's distracting and can be seen as rude, making the other person feel undervalued.

Strategy 5: Cathartic exhale or breathing

A clear sign of stress in someone is when they puff out their cheeks and then exhale deeply through pursed lips, almost like they're whistling, but with no sound. It's similar to blowing out a candle, but with more air held in the cheeks. This is a common visual cue, especially in tense or stressful situations. You can actually use this same technique to help someone calm down. By using an exhale or slowing down your own breathing, you can subtly encourage the other person to do the same. This works because of mirror neurons, which are brain cells that activate both when you perform an action and when you see someone else doing it. Simply put, when you show calm and controlled behaviour, others might naturally follow suit, helping them to relax as well.

Strategy 6: Raising or arching of the eyebrows

Some behaviour that moves upwards can signal a positive emotion – this is often referred to as 'gravity-defying behaviour'. For example, raising your hands in celebration when you win, or jumping up and down out of excitement (though most adults don't do this as often, they likely remember it from childhood). This upward movement can also be seen in a person's face. When someone is happy to see you, their eyebrows often arch upwards and if you're listening to a story that excites or resonates with you, your own eyebrows might lift in response. You can also use your face to express positive emotions. If you're listening to a story and you want to reinforce positive feelings, lift your eyebrows slightly to show engagement.

You can also use your eyebrows for emphasis in more serious or empathetic situations. When listening to a negative or intense story, raising or furrowing your eyebrows slightly can help to convey understanding and empathy. In serious conversations, let your face and eyebrow behaviour reflect your attentiveness and the gravity of the moment, showing that you are fully engaged and recognize the seriousness of the topic.

Strategy 7: The smile

Your smile can be a powerful tool to help guide a conversation. When used thoughtfully, it can help to establish rapport, ease tension and create a more open, positive atmosphere.

To begin, ensure that your smile is genuine. A true smile, known as the Duchenne smile, involves both the mouth and the eyes – look for the slight wrinkles around your eyes as you smile. This will make you appear more authentic and approachable. A genuine smile can help put the other person at ease, making them more likely to open up.

In a difficult conversation, you can also use your smile to soften the tone. If things start to feel tense, try offering a warm smile to signal understanding and empathy. A smile can help defuse negative emotions. If the conversation is becoming too heated, a gentle smile can show that you're not defensive and that you're open to listening. It helps create a sense of safety, allowing both parties to communicate more effectively and calmly. However, be mindful of timing – don't force a smile in a serious moment as this can come across as insincere.

Finally, be aware of how long your smile lasts. A quick, fleeting smile might signal discomfort, while a longer, more sustained smile helps convey genuine warmth and engagement.

Conclusion

Nonverbal communication is one of the most effective tools we have to make others feel at ease. By adjusting our body language, we can create a more comfortable atmosphere and foster better conversations. This tool doesn't just benefit others; it can help us too. If you're feeling uncomfortable, take a moment to assess the situation around you. Sometimes, taking a small step back can make a big difference in how you feel, or shifting your eye contact can boost your self-assurance. Body language is a powerful resource – use it, embrace it and let it work for you in every interaction.

Conclusion

Behaviour isn't just important; it's everything. It's the foundation of how we connect, communicate and grow, both at work and in life. The way we behave shapes how others perceive us, how we collaborate and, ultimately, what we achieve.

When our behaviour aligns with our values and goals, the people who surround us and the context, communication becomes clearer and relationships strengthen. If you present yourself with confidence and authenticity you create an environment where challenges are easier to face and opportunities feel within reach. If you observe others, you will understand more than just their words. If you conduct meetings with care, you will create clarity, focus and respect. If you lead in a conscious and focused way, you will not only help yourself, but you will also help your team and the company. And if you stay calm in challenging situations, you will think more clearly, respond more effectively and help others do the same.

Not all situations we encounter at work are easy, but we have the power to influence the outcome by choosing to act with intention and care. Observe, choose behaviour, reflect, evaluate and adapt.

Behaviour isn't something fixed, it's something we can work on. And when we do, with awareness and intention, the results are powerful. By reflecting on our actions, listening to feedback and being open to change, we become more adaptable to the situations that life and work throw at us. We can improve those moments that feel a bit awkward by challenging ourselves to step up and take action to make the situation better.

Improving your behaviour isn't just about reacting to others. It's also about reacting towards yourself. What drives me? How do I show up? What is my effect? How do I react? What can I adjust? These small, conscious shifts create a difference, and that's what you should aim for. By understanding how we behave, we gain the ability to refine and adjust our approach, which makes us more adaptable and effective in our personal and professional lives.

We can be better, more effective and even happier.

And yes, that's a bold statement, but I see it every day.

Because when people take a closer look at themselves, change their behaviour and start seeing results, they experience just how much is possible and they realize how powerful that change can be. There's a kind of magic in that change. When you realize there's more in you than you thought there was, it feels incredible. When you enhance your behaviour and suddenly what you aimed for is actually happening, it creates this powerful sense of fulfilment. That change in behaviour, however small it is, can come from an inspirational talk, training or even from some practical steps that you've found in this book.

So, take a moment and thank yourself. You've taken the time to read this book. Maybe you read just a few chapters, maybe you read them all. In the end you took the time to invest in yourself and that matters. And now, the next step is simple:

Put it into practice.

Use what you've learned and make the choice to consistently apply it in your daily life. This is how you can truly transform your communication, relationships and overall success.

Shakespeare said, 'To be or not to be; that is the question.' Inspired by his words, I'd like to end with my own twist: 'To do or not to do; that is the question!'

Good luck!

Afterword

This book is never truly finished because, every day, people ask new questions and offer fresh perspectives. There's always more to discover, explore and share. Our understanding of behaviour is constantly evolving and the conversations around it are ongoing. But at some point, you must pause and reach the end. My goal in writing this was to create a practical guide, something that would offer value to you in your journey of self-improvement and understanding of behaviour. Now, I'd love to hear from you – were there any questions I didn't cover? Is there something you'd like to dive deeper into?

I would love to hear about your experiences as you begin to try out the strategies from this book. How have they worked for you? What challenges have you faced and what successes have you seen? I'm eager to hear your thoughts and would love to support you further in your journey. If you're ready for more coaching or need guidance on how to apply the insights from this book to your specific situation, don't hesitate to reach out.

I truly hope that this book has provided you with that little nudge to take action. Whether it's starting a conversation about behaviour with others, stepping outside your comfort zone or focusing on your own personal growth, I want this to be the spark that sets you on a path of effective behaviour. While I would have loved the opportunity to work with each of you personally, because I know everyone has their own unique needs and ways of fine-tuning their behaviour, think of this book as just the starting point. It's the foundation, and now it's up to you to build on it.

Contact details: amo@behaviourcompany.eu

References

Introduction

This chapter is based on ideas contained in the following article: Joe Navarro and Anne-Maartje Oud, 'The Helicopter Technique Metaphor', *Psychology Today*, May 2020, www.psychologytoday.com/us/blog/spycatcher/202005/the-helicopter-technique-metaphor (archived at https://perma.cc/5J2G-4FY9)

Part One

Adam, H and Galinsky, A D (2012) Enclothed Cognition, *Journal of Experimental Social Psychology*, 48 (4) pp. 918–25

BBNC Uitgevers (2019) *999 Questions to Ask Yourself*, Gouda

Blom, R (2023) New smoking cessation campaign asks for understanding from non-smokers, Adformatie, 27 December, www.adformatie.nl/communicatie/campagnes/nieuwe-stoppen-met-roken-campagne-vraagt-begrip-van-de-niet-roker (archived at https://perma.cc/J2PM-MZ5A)

Canfield, J and Hansen, M V (2000) *Chicken Soup for the Soul*, London: Vermillion

CNN (2022) Michelle Obama has advice for girl's [sic] battling self-doubt, YouTube, 21 November, www.youtube.com/watch?v=bzNke_GYGHg

Navarro, J (2021) *Be Exceptional: Master the five traits that set extraordinary people apart*, William Morrow

Part Two

Cuddy, A (2012) Your body language may shape who you are, TED, YouTube, 1 October, www.youtube.com/watch?v=Ks-_Mh1QhMc (archived at https://perma.cc/BC9L-643E)

Navarro, J (2018) *The Dictionary of Body Language: A field guide to human behavior*, London: HarperCollins, 51

REFERENCES

Watzlawick, P, Bavelas, J and Jackson, D J (1967) *Pragmatics of Human Communication: A study of interactional patterns, pathologies, and paradoxes*, New York: W.W. Norton & Company

Part Three

Fresco, L (2009) Louise Fresco on feeding the whole world, YouTube, https://www.youtube.com/watch?v=UZmXwOgNq7c&t=1027s (archived at https://perma.cc/2T2A-QLDQ)

Streep, P (2023) 'Why the "still-face" experiment was a game-changer', *Psychology Today*, 10 July, www.psychologytoday.com/gb/blog/tech-support/202307/why-the-still-face-experiment-was-a-game-changer (archived at https://perma.cc/S5EF-K6CU)

Part Four

Goleman, D (2017) *Leadership that Gets Results*, Boston: Harvard Business Review Press

Hamilton, I (1921) *The Soul and Body of an Army*, London: Edward Arnold & Co

Hersey, P and Blanchard, K H (1986) *The Situational Leader* (4th edn), Prentice Hall & IBD

Lee Hotz, R (1999) Mars probe lost due to simple math error, *Los Angeles Times*, 1 October, www.latimes.com/archives/la-xpm-1999-oct-01-mn-17288-story.html (archived at https://perma.cc/ZZ63-VD4K)

McGregor, D (1960) *The Human Side of Enterprise*, New York: McGraw-Hill

Meyer, E (2014) *The Culture Map: Breaking through the invisible boundaries of global business*, New York: PublicAffairs

Mindtools Content Team (n.d.) Dealing with a wide span of control, Mindtools, www.mindtools.com/ao63g8c/dealing-with-a-wide-span-of-control (archived at https://perma.cc/CH5T-E5XJ)

Navarro, J and Oud, A (2021) The importance of validation, *Psychology Today*, 21 June, www.psychologytoday.com/us/blog/spycatcher/202106/the-importance-of-validation (archived at https://perma.cc/DA9V-RNXT)

Radcliffe, S (2012) *Leadership: Plain and Simple*, Harlow: Pearson Education

Twenge, J M (2023) *Generations: The real differences between Gen Z, Millennials, Gen X, Boomers, and Silents—and what they mean for the future*, New York: Atria Books

Part Five

De Becker, G (2000) *The Gift of Fear: Survival signals that protect us from violence*, London: Bloomsbury Publishing

Navarro, J (2014) *Dangerous Personalities: An FBI profiler shows you how to identify and protect yourself from harmful people*, Rodale

Voss, C and Raz, T (2016) *Never Split the Difference: Negotiating as if your life depended on it*, New York: Harper Business

Further reading

Bavelas, J, Gerwing, J and Healing, S (2014) 7 hand and facial gestures in conversational interaction, in Thomas M Holtgraves (ed.), *The Oxford Handbook of Language and Social Psychology*, Oxford Library of Psychology

BetterHealth Channel (n.d.) Breathing to reduce stress, Victoria State Government Department of Health, https://www.betterhealth.vic.gov.au/health/healthyliving/breathing-to-reduce-stress (archived at https://perma.cc/57BN-QC5C)

Boyd, C, Hartzell and S (2023) McGregor's Theory X & Theory Y: definition & manager types, Study.com, November, https://study.com/learn/lesson/theory-x-theory-y-management-types-examples.html (archived at https://perma.cc/SGD6-SJPT)

Bulkeley, G (1895) *Will and Doom: Or the miseries of Connecticut by and under a usurped and arbitrary power*, Hartford, CT: Press of the Case, Lockwood & Brainard Company

Carnegie, D (1936) *How to Win Friends and Influence People*, New York: Simon & Schuster

Cialdini, R B (2006) *Influence: The psychology of persuasion*, New York: Harper Business

Cialdini, R B (2016) *Pre-Suasion: A revolutionary way to influence and persuade*, New York: Simon & Schuster

Covey, S R (1989) *The 7 Habits of Highly Effective People: Powerful lessons in personal change*, New York: Free Press

Covey, S R (2004) *The 8th Habit: From effectiveness to greatness*, New York: Free Press

Cuddy, A (2015) *Presence: Bringing your boldest self to your biggest challenges*, New York: Little, Brown Spark

Darwin, C (1872) *The Expression of the Emotions in Man and Animals*, London: John Murray

Ekman, P (2000) *De Leugen Ontmaskerd* (Dutch edition of *Telling Lies*), Nieuwezijds (Amsterdam)

Ekman, P (2004) *Gegrepen Door Emoties* (Dutch edition of *Emotions Revealed*), Nieuwezijds (Amsterdam)

Gandini E (dir.) (2023) After work [documentary] https://www.imdb.com/title/tt10400026/ (archived at https://perma.cc/Y54H-TZ97)

Greene, R (2013) *Mastery*, New York: Penguin Books

Hadnagy, C (2018) *Social Engineering: The science of human hacking*, Hoboken, NJ: Wiley

Hadnagy, C and Schulman, S (2021) *Human Hacking: Win friends, influence people, and leave them better off for having met you*, New York: Harper Business

Hare, R D (1999) *Without Conscience: The disturbing world of the psychopaths among us*, New York: Guilford Press

Hare, R D and Babiak, P (2006) *Snakes in Suits: When psychopaths go to work*, New York: Harper Business

Hollis, R (2019) *Girl, Stop Apologizing: A shame-free plan for embracing and achieving your goals*, Nashville: HarperCollins Leadership

Kilner, J M and Lemon, R N (2013) What we know currently about mirror neurons, National Library of Medicine, 2 December

King, S (2000) *On Writing: A memoir of the craft*, New York: Scribner

Klumpers, K (1991) *Mooi weertje vandaag!*, Amsterdam: Boom

Kreisman, J J and Straus, H (2010) *I Hate You – Don't Leave Me: Understanding the borderline personality*, New York: Penguin Books

Marino, S (2025) 180+ strategy-changing digital marketing statistics for 2025, WordStream, www.wordstream.com/blog/ws/2022/04/19/digital-marketing-statistics (archived at https://perma.cc/T5SX-KHQB)

Martinuzzi, B (2023) How to prepare a last-minute presentation efficiently, American Express, 11 July, www.americanexpress.com/en-us/business/trends-and-insights/articles/make-a-good-presentation-when-theres-no-time-to-prepare/ (archived at https://perma.cc/6TV9-2FAN)

Meyer, E (2014) *The Culture Map: Breaking through the invisible boundaries of global business*, New York: PublicAffairs

Mlodinow, L (2012) *Subliminal: How your unconscious mind rules your behavior*, New York: Vintage

Mlodinow, L (2022) *Emotional: How feelings shape our thinking*, New York: Pantheon

Mohr, T (2015) *Playing Big: Practical wisdom for women who want to speak up, create, and lead*, New York: Avery

Morris, D (1967) *De Naakte Aap*, Utrecht: Bruna

Morris, D (1969) *The Human Zoo*, New York: McGraw-Hill

Morris, D (1979) *Gestures: Their origins and distribution*, London: Jonathan Cape

Morris, D (1994) *The Human Animal: A personal view of the human species*, London: BBC Books

Morris, D (2002) *Peoplewatching: The Desmond Morris guide to body language*, London: Vintage

Navarro, J (2008) *What Every BODY is Saying: An Ex-FBI agent's guide to speed-reading people*, New York: HarperCollins

Navarro, J (2010) Body language of the hands, *Psychology Today*, 20 January, www.psychologytoday.com/gb/blog/spycatcher/201001/body-language-of-the-hands

Navarro, J (2016) The paranoid partner, *Psychology Today*, 14 March, www.psychologytoday.com/us/blog/spycatcher/201603/the-paranoid-partner (archived at https://perma.cc/VLB7-TE3M)

Navarro, J (2018) *The Dictionary of Body Language: A field guide to human behavior*, London: HarperCollins, p. 51

Navarro, J (2018) *The Dictionary of Body Language: A field guide to human behavior*, London: Thorsons

Navarro, J (2021) *Be Exceptional: Master the five traits that set extraordinary people apart*, New York: William Morrow

Navarro, J (n.d.) *Clues to Deceit: A practical list*, publisher not specified

Navarro, J and Oud, A (2020) Conducting difficult interviews or conversations, *Psychology Today*, 1 February, www.psychologytoday.com/us/blog/spycatcher/202002/conducting-difficult-interviews-or-conversations

Navarro, J and Oud, A (2023) 20 tips for successful meetings, *Psychology Today*, 26 March, www.psychologytoday.com/us/blog/spycatcher/202303/20-tips-for-successful-meetings

Navarro, J and Oud, A (2023) 20 ways to de-escalate emotional situations, *Psychology Today*, 17 July, www.psychologytoday.com/us/blog/spycatcher/202307/20-tips-for-de-escalating-emotional-situations (archived at https://perma.cc/G46J-QWYF)

Navarro, J and Poynter, T S (2011) *Louder Than Words: Take your career from average to exceptional with the hidden power of nonverbal intelligence*, New York: Harper Business

Navarro, J and Poynter, T S (2018) *Dangerous Personalities: An FBI profiler shows you how to identify and protect yourself from harmful people*, New York: Rodale Books

Noah, J, Dravida, S, Zhang, X, Yahil, S and Hirsch, J (2016) Neural correlates of conflict between gestures and words: A domain-specific role for a temporal-parietal complex, *PLoS ONE*, 12 (3), October

Ofman, D (1992) *Bezieling en kwaliteit in organisaties*, Utrecht: Servire

Ofman, D (2022) *Fancy Meeting Me Here: Using core quadrants to discover and develop your core qualities* (1st edn), Zaltbommel: Core Quality International

Purves, D, Augustine, G J, Fitzpatrick, D et al (eds) *Neuroscience* (4th edn), Sinauer Associates, Sunderland (MA), www.ncbi.nlm.nih.gov/books/NBK10799/ (archived at https://perma.cc/9CJ4-WGED)

Robbins, S P and Judge, T A (2020) *Gedrag in Organisaties*, Amsterdam: Pearson Benelux

RTL News (2022) Criticism from all sides about John de Mol's statements about The Voice, RTL, 21 January, www.rtl.nl/nieuws/nederland/artikel/5282739/van-alle-kanten-kritiek-op-uitspraken-john-de-mol-over (archived at https://perma.cc/Q3D9-3NJ3)

Schafer, J R and Navarro, J (2023) *Advanced Interviewing Techniques: Proven strategies for law enforcement, military, and security personnel*, Springfield, IL: Charles C Thomas Publisher

Steptoe, A, Gibson, E L, Vuononvirta, R, Williams, E, Hamer, M, Rycroft, J, Erusalimsky, J D and Wardle, J (2007) The effects of tea on psychophysiological stress responsivity and post-stress recovery: a randomised double-blind trial, *Psychopharmacology*, 190 (1), pp. 81–89

Swaab, D and Schutten, J P (n.d.) *Jij Bent Je Brein*, Amsterdam: publisher not specified

Swaab, D and Schutten, J P (n.d.) *Wij Zijn Ons Brein*, Amsterdam: publisher not specified

Sutton, R I (2007) *The No Asshole Rule: Building a civilized workplace and surviving one that isn't*, New York: Business Plus

Voss, C and Raz, T (2016) *Never Split the Difference: Negotiating as if your life depended on it*, New York: Harper Business

Wallace, D (2005) *I Can't Believe You Just Said That*, London: Ebury Press

Wallace, D (2006) *Yes Man*, London: Ebury Press

From 4 December 2025 the EU Responsible Person (GPSR) is:
eucomply oÜ, Pärnu mnt. 139b – 14, 11317 Tallinn, Estonia
www.eucompliancepartner.com